Unit B

Weather Station

Instruments and Observations

I WONDER

Science begins with wondering. What do you wonder about when you see places with weather like the ones shown?

Work with a partner to make a list of weather questions you may have. Be ready to share your list with the rest of the class.

Death Valley, California

Bison in a winter storm in Montana

I PLAN

You may have asked questions such as these as you wondered about weather. Scientists also ask questions. Then they plan ways to help them find answers to their questions. Now you and your classmates can plan how you will investigate weather.

My Science Log

- Why does it feel warmer on some days than on others?

- How can weather be predicted?

- Why is it important to know what the weather will be?

- Is weather affected by air pollution?

With Your Class

Plan how your class will use the activities and readings from the **I Investigate** part of this unit.

On Your Own

There are many ways to learn about weather. Following are some things you can do to explore weather by yourself or with some classmates. Some explorations may take longer to do than others. Look over the suggestions and choose . . .

- **Places to Visit**
- **Projects to Do**
- **Books to Read**

PLACES TO VISIT

TELEVISION STATION

Contact the weather reporter at a local television station. Find out when you can visit. Then, with an adult, go to the television station and talk with the weather reporter. Ask questions and take notes about the equipment and maps he or she uses. Also find out how he or she gets weather information. Make a bulletin-board display that shows what you discovered from your visit.

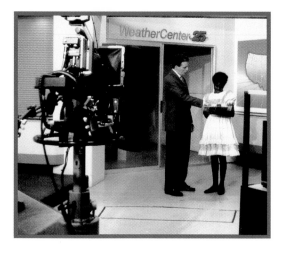

HISTORICAL SOCIETY

Visit a historical society or a library that has a photograph collection. Look at photographs of major storms that have happened in your area in the past ten years. Make a time line of these big storms. Share your time line with a family member.

SERVICE STATION

Visit a local service station or motor vehicle inspection station. Ask the workers how they test the exhaust emissions of cars and trucks. Find out what types of air pollutants they test for. Ask what can be done to correct an emission problem. Perhaps they will have brochures to give you. Write an article about your visit. Find out if your school newspaper would like to publish your article.

PROJECTS TO DO

SCIENCE FAIR PROJECT

Design a weather station. Discuss your ideas with your teacher. Do research to find out how to make weather instruments. If your teacher agrees, build your weather station. Then use your instruments to check the weather for one month, and record your findings in a chart. Display your weather instruments and chart at your school science fair.

WEATHER RESEARCHER

Be a weather researcher. Find out the highest and lowest temperatures in your area for each year since you were born. Make a poster that summarizes what you found out.

WEATHER SAYINGS

It seems as if everybody talks about the weather. Some people use "sayings" to tell something about the weather. One weather saying is "If the cows lie down, it will rain soon." Talk to people in your area. What weather sayings do they use? After you have collected several weather sayings, do some research. Ask a librarian to help you find out how your sayings began and why people use them. Then make a drawing for each weather saying. Present your weather sayings to your classmates.

BOOKS TO READ

Water's Way

by Lisa Westberg Peters (Arcade Publishing, 1991).
What can be hard, soft, or liquid? What can run down your window or run down a mountain? You're right if you guessed *water*. When the weather changes, the water outside also changes. Spend the day with Tony in this book as he waits for snow. Clouds form. Raindrops splash. Finally the air is cold enough to turn the water into snow. Will it snow so Tony can use his sled?

Weather Words and What They Mean

by Gail Gibbons (Holiday House, 1990). There are many words to describe weather. Many you know. Some weather words, like *clouds,* name things that are easy to see, but others, like *air pressure,* do not. Did you know there are different kinds of clouds and different kinds of winds? This book will help you understand the weather and the words that describe it.

More Books to Read

A Rainy Day

by Sandra Markle (Orchard Books, 1993). If there is no thunder or lightning, you can put on a raincoat and boots and go outside to watch the rain. What happens to the water after the rain stops? Read this book to find out.

Linnea's Almanac

by Christina Bjork (Farrar, Straus & Giroux, 1989). Linnea is a young girl who lives in a city. She loves animals and plants. In this book, she shares her activities and observations with you. You will have fun making crafts from this book.

Weather Forecasting

by Gail Gibbons (Macmillan, 1987), Outstanding Science Trade Book. Weather forecasters are people who tell us about the weather and what our weather will be. They use tools from balloons to computers so they can track weather changes. In this book, you will learn how this is done and why it is important.

When the Rain Stops

by Sheila Cole (Lothrop, Lee & Shepard, 1992). When the rain starts, Leila and her dad go inside, but it comes in through a hole in the roof! After the rain, the world looks and smells different.

INVESTIGATE

To find answers to their questions, scientists read, think, talk to others, and do experiments. Their investigations often lead to new questions. In this unit, you will have many chances to think and work like a scientist. How will you find answers to questions you asked?

▶ INTERPRETING DATA   Data is information given to you or information that you gather during activities. When you interpret data, you decide what it means.

▶ MEASURING   Measuring is a way to observe and compare things accurately. When you measure, you often use an instrument, such as a ruler or a balance.

▶ COMMUNICATING   When you communicate, you give information. In science, you communicate by showing results from an activity in an organized way—for example, in a chart. Then you and other people can interpret the results.

Are you ready to begin?

FORMATIONS

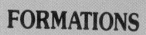

CUMULONIMBUS

ALTOSTRATUS

CUMULUS

APPROXIMATE ALTITUDE
IN FEET

FOG

SECTIONS

Weather Measurements

▲ **Snowstorm in New York City**

Suppose you went to a doctor's office for a checkup and instead of taking your temperature, the staff said they were just going to guess. Would you want them to care of you? Of course not. You'd want them to take an exact measurement. That way they would have the information they need.

Another time when people need to have exact measurements is when they predict the weather. To do that, they need to know the exact temperature, the exact amount of moisture in the air and the exact amount of rain that falls. In this section, you'll learn about some instruments that are used to make weather measurements. Keep notes in your Science Log.

1 MEASURING AIR TEMPERATURE

"It's warm today," you say to a friend as sweat drips from your face.

"Not as warm as it was yesterday," your friend replies.

"Are you sure? Today seems warmer to me," you say.

"Yes," your friend answers. "I know for sure."

How can your friend be so sure? Can you guess the temperature? The following activities will help you understand the importance of air temperature in predicting weather.

What's Wrong Here?

Even though you are just beginning to study weather, you already know much about the subject.

Look at the pictures on this page. Pick out what's wrong with each one. Be ready to discuss your answers with another person.

THINK ABOUT IT

How did you decide what was wrong with each of the pictures on this page? What did you need to know about weather to decide?

Making a Thermometer

A *thermometer* is an instrument that measures temperature. In this activity, you'll make a simple thermometer and learn how to read it.

DO THIS

1 Add water to the bottle until it is nearly full. Add several drops of the food coloring to turn the water red.

2 Put the straw in the bottle, with about three-fourths sticking out of the top. Use the clay to seal the opening around the straw.

MATERIALS

- 1–L plastic bottle
- water
- red food coloring
- clear drinking straw
- clay
- clear plastic cup
- dropper
- ruler
- Science Log data sheet

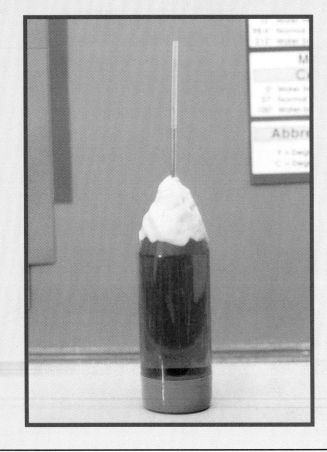

3 Fill the cup half full with water. Add red food coloring to color the water. Use the dropper to add colored water to the straw until the water level is above the top of the clay seal.

4 Use the ruler to measure the water level above the clay seal. Record the measurement. You have made a thermometer.

5 Take your thermometer to different places inside your
school and outdoors. Set the thermometer down at each
place and leave it there for ten minutes or so. When
the water level in your thermometer changes, measure
the new level. Make sure you don't squeeze the bottle
while you're measuring. Record the measurement
and the name of the place where you took it. Take
measurements in at least five different places.

THINK AND WRITE

1. What did you notice about the water level when the
   temperature changed? List the places and their
   temperatures in order from the warmest to the coldest.

2. What information did your thermometer give you?

3. What information about the temperature could you not
   get from your thermometer? Tell why.

Making Exact Measurements

In the last activity, you learned how to find out whether one place was warmer or cooler than another. Now you'll use a thermometer in the same places to make temperature measurements. You'll also find out why it's important to use exact measurements.

DO THIS

MATERIALS
- thermometer
- Science Log data sheet

❶ Take the thermometer to the same places as in the last activity. Measure the exact temperature in each place and record the readings.

❷ Compare the data you collected in the last activity with the exact temperature readings you just made.

3 Compare your findings with those of one other group. Are your findings the same or different? Give reasons for differences you may have.

THINK AND WRITE

1. List the places in order from the warmest to the coldest. Are they in the same order as in the last activity? Explain any differences.

2. What does the thermometer in this activity have that the thermometer you made does not have?

3. Give an example of a time when you would need an exact temperature reading and an example of a time when you wouldn't need an exact reading.

4. **COMMUNICATING** Suppose you wanted to write a letter to your cousin in another state to tell him about the weather where you live. Why would it be better to use thermometer readings than the data from a water bottle thermometer?

LESSON 1 REVIEW

1 Why is it important for a thermometer to have a scale with numbers on it?

2 Why do people need to measure exact temperatures?

 SEASONS

Do you have a favorite season? Maybe you like the summer because it's warm enough for you to go swimming. You may like the winter because it gets cold and snows. Or maybe you don't have a favorite season because you live someplace where the weather is nearly the same for most of the year.

Different Seasons

The kind of weather you have at different times of the year depends on where you live. These photos show the different seasons at a stream in the Morristown National Historic Park in New Jersey.

▲ In winter, snow is common and the tree branches are bare.

▲ In spring, the trees along the stream begin to bud.

▲ In summer, the leaves on the trees shade the stream from the sun.

▲ In autumn, the leaves change color and fall to the ground.

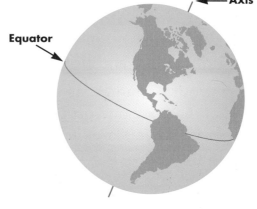

Look at the drawing. You can see a line that goes around the middle of the Earth. It stands for an imaginary line that divides Earth into a northern half and a southern half. This imaginary line is called the *equator.*

There is also an imaginary line that runs from the North Pole through the Earth to the South Pole. This is called Earth's *axis.* Earth is tilted on its axis. It remains tilted in the same direction as it moves around the sun.

THINK ABOUT IT

What is your favorite season? Why?

Tilt Makes the Difference

What causes the different seasons on Earth? The following activity will help you understand one important cause.

MATERIALS

- large book
- graph paper
- transparent tape
- flashlight
- 2 markers (black and red)
- Science Log data sheet

DO THIS

1. Tape a sheet of graph paper onto the book, and place the book on the floor. Darken the room. Shine the flashlight straight down on the paper. The beam of light should make a small circle at the center of the paper. If the circle is too big, lower the flashlight. (Don't move the flashlight again until you complete step 4.)

2. Have a partner use the black marker to trace around the circle. Note the brightness of the light on the squares.

3. Have your partner raise one end of the book and graph paper while you keep the flashlight aimed the same way as before.

4. Have your partner use the red marker to trace the shape of the light on the graph paper. Again note the brightness of the light on the squares.

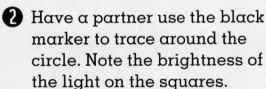

THINK AND WRITE

1. How many squares were inside the black line? How many were inside the red line? Why were the numbers of squares different? In which outline was a single square brighter?

2. Suppose the graph paper stood for Earth and the flashlight stood for the sun. Which area do you think would have warmer weather? Why?

Sunny Side Up

In the last activity, you explored Earth's tilt. Now you will see how that helps cause the seasons.

Think about what sunlight does. During the day, when the sun shines, the temperature is warmer than at night. The sun shining on Earth gives us light and heat.

Remember the light that you observed on the graph paper in the last activity? The light on the paper was brighter when it was spread over fewer squares. This happened when the flashlight shined on the paper directly. When the paper was tilted, the light was weaker.

During the summer in the United States, the sun shines on the northern half of Earth more directly than in the winter. We have more hours of daylight and warmer temperatures.

The northern half of Earth has winter when the sun is shining more directly on Earth's southern half. It is summer for the people who live south of the equator. In the United States, the winter months are December, January, and February. Those are summer months in southern Africa. In southern Africa, what season is it during June, July, and August?

As Earth revolves, or moves around the sun, the seasons change. On the next two pages, notice the pictures of Earth's position.

December 21

▲ Northern Hemisphere: Sledding is fun.

Southern Hemisphere: A trip to the beach. ▼

Most people in states like New York, Minnesota, and Montana wouldn't dream of swimming outside in late December. But that's exactly what people do in Australia and South America. You can even go swimming in the southern part of the United States in winter. This is because the closer you are to the equator, the warmer it stays year-round. The North and South Poles are far away from the equator. It's never very warm at those places.

March 20

▲ Northern Hemisphere: Daffodils bloom in the spring.

When March comes, the sun shines almost equally on the northern and southern halves of Earth. In the northern half, the weather is turning warm. Spring is beginning. In the southern half, the days are growing cooler. Autumn has come.

◄ Southern Hemisphere: Fruits like Litchi nuts are ripe in autumn.

Once again, neither half of Earth is receiving more direct sunlight than the other half. The days are getting cooler in the northern half and warmer in the southern half.

Northern Hemisphere: Leaves fall off many trees in autumn. ▶

Southern Hemisphere: A cool treat is good on a spring day. ▼

Toward the end of June, the northern half of Earth receives more direct sunlight and summer begins. At the same time, winter is beginning in the southern half of Earth.

▲ Northern Hemisphere: Picnics in summer.
▼ Southern Hemisphere: Snowballs in winter.

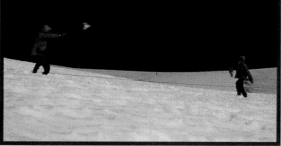

THINK ABOUT IT

Suppose you were taking a trip from Georgia to Canada in April. What kinds of clothes would you pack? Explain your answer.

How Hot? How Cold?

Different parts of the world have different temperatures. Some places get very hot. Other places get very cold. Where is it hottest? Where is it coldest? Let's take a trip around the world to find out.

▲ The hottest place in the United States is Death Valley in California. Temperatures in Death Valley have gone above 54 degrees Celsius (130 degrees Fahrenheit).

▲ In the country of Egypt in Africa, it gets even hotter than in Death Valley. In hot countries like Egypt, people try to stay out of the sun in the middle of the day.

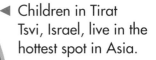

◄ Children in Tirat Tsvi, Israel, live in the hottest spot in Asia.

▲ Europe's hottest place is Seville, Spain.

The hottest place in South America is in Argentina in the province of Salta. ▶

▲ In the winter, children have to dress very warmly in northern Canada. Temperatures there drop to a very cold 62 degrees Celsius below zero (80 degrees Fahrenheit below zero).

▲ The coldest place on Earth is in the heart of Antarctica. Antarctica is the continent that surrounds the South Pole. Russian scientists work high on the ice at a place called Vostok. Temperatures there have fallen to more than 88 degrees Celsius below zero (127 degrees Fahrenheit below zero). The scientists at Vostok are studying the weather. They are also drilling a deep hole through ice layers that are at least 3,700 meters (about 12,140 feet) deep. They will study ice samples to learn about changes in the climate of Antarctica over many thousands of years.

QUICK CHECK

LESSON 2 REVIEW

❶ Find Canada, Antarctica, and Egypt on a globe or world map. Then tell what the location of a place has to do with its temperature.

❷ How do Earth's tilt and Earth's movement around the sun cause the seasons?

3 WATER VAPOR AND HUMIDITY

It's a very warm day. The sky is cloudy. You walk out of your front door, and it almost feels as if you're stepping into the shower. But it isn't raining. Why does the air feel so damp? In this lesson, you'll discover answers to questions like this about water vapor and humidity.

ACTIVITY

Does a Glass Sweat?

Think back to a time when you tried to pick up a glass of milk or water, but your hand slipped off the glass. Why was the glass slippery? This activity will help clear up the mystery.

MATERIALS
- 2 clear plastic cups
- ice
- water
- ruler
- thermometer
- Science Log data sheet

DO THIS

1 Fill one cup with water and ice and one with just water. Set the cups on a table about 10 cm apart.

2 Observe what happens to the outside of the cups. Feel the air close to each cup. How is the air temperature near each cup different from the air temperature in the rest of the room?

3 Use the thermometer to measure the temperature of the water in each cup and the air temperature. How is the temperature of each cup of water different from the air temperature?

THINK AND WRITE

Compare what happened on the outside of the two cups.

Water in the Air

What is water vapor? What is humidity? How can we find out about them?

Water in the form of a gas is called *water vapor*. Air contains water vapor. The amount of water vapor in the air is called *humidity* (hyoo MID uh tee). All air does not have the same humidity. Air can hold only a certain amount of water vapor. The amount depends on the temperature of the air.

In the activity you just did, the air near the cup of ice water was cooler than the air in the rest of the room. Cool air cannot hold as much water vapor as warm air. If warm air cools, it cannot hold as much water vapor as before. So some of the water vapor comes out of the air. This water vapor turns into liquid water called *condensation* (kahn duhn SAY shuhn). The water on the outside of the ice-water cup was condensation. Water vapor is said to *condense* when it turns into liquid water.

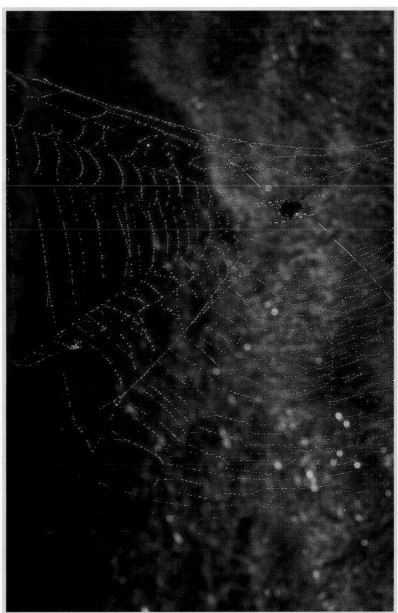

Dew on a spider web ▶

You've probably walked through grass early in the morning and found it covered with water drops. These water drops, called *dew*, come from water vapor in the cool morning air. Dew forms in a way similar to the way in which condensation forms on the side of a cup. At night, Earth's surface loses heat. The layer of air near the surface becomes cooler. The water vapor in the air begins to condense onto grass, leaves, car windows, bicycles, and other objects. If the air is cold enough, ice crystals form. These crystals are called *frost*. As the air begins to warm up, the dew or frost evaporates, becoming water vapor again.

▲ **Morning dew on the grass**

THINK ABOUT IT

1. Compare what happens when water vapor condenses and when water evaporates.

2. Look at the pictures below. What would happen to the glass in each of these places? Explain your answer.

When Is Humidity Different?

Now let's look at humidity again.

DO THIS

1 Use the marker to write your name on the outside of the metal can.

2 Half fill the can with water that is about the same temperature as the air in the room. Measure the water temperature with the thermometer, and record it.

3 Add 2 or 3 ice cubes to the water. Slowly stir the water with the spoon.

4 Have a partner observe your name on the can. When it becomes blurred with a thin layer of water, measure the water temperature again, and record it.

5 Repeat this activity outside on days when the weather is different. Also record what the weather is like (clear, cloudy, rainy, and so on). Compare your results.

MATERIALS
- metal can
- marker
- water
- thermometer
- ice cubes
- spoon
- Science Log data sheet

THINK AND WRITE

1. In what ways did your results change on different days?

2. **INTERPRETING DATA** In this activity, you gathered data, or information. By itself, the data didn't mean anything. But when you figured out what the data meant, you could reach a conclusion about humidity. What data did you gather? What did the data tell you about humidity?

It's Not the Heat—It's the Humidity

Have you ever noticed that on some very hot days, you still feel comfortable? On other days when it's the same temperature, you feel sticky and sweaty. The reason for this difference is the humidity.

One way your body is cooled is through sweating. If your body gets too warm, it produces sweat. The water in the sweat on your skin turns into water vapor and goes into the air. The water vapor takes with it some of the heat from your body.

You know that warm air can hold more water vapor than cool air. But even warm air has limits. When the humidity is high, the air can't hold much more water vapor. So your sweat can't cool you. Its water stays on your skin as a liquid. You feel sweaty and hot.

QUICK CHECK

LESSON 3 REVIEW

Suppose it's a hot and humid day. You're all sweaty and the lemonade you're drinking has water condensed on the outside of the glass. What are the similarities between you and the glass? What are the differences?

4 CLOUDS AND PRECIPITATION

You start out on your way to school one morning and look up at the sky. There are several clouds in the sky. You decide to go back home for your raincoat. All day you wait for it to begin raining, but it never does. You wonder why. Don't clouds in the sky always mean rain? In this lesson, you'll find out about clouds and weather.

Predicting the Weather from Clouds

Have you noticed that the clouds in the sky don't always look the same? What is a cloud? Read on to find out.

A cloud doesn't look like a pool of water. But that's what it is. The drops of water in a cloud are very small and far apart. Clouds form when warm, moist air is forced upward by cooler, drier air. As warm air is pushed upward, it cools. Remember that cooler air can hold less water vapor than warm air. So when the warm air cools, some of its water vapor condenses into tiny water drops. The tiny drops form clouds. Sometimes the drops clump together and fall. Then we see them as rain, snow, sleet, or hail.

You probably know that clouds come in many different shapes. The shape of a cloud and its height in the sky are clues to the kind of weather that's on the way. There are three main kinds of clouds. Let's look at some clouds and find out what weather comes with them.

Stratus Clouds

If you see a blanket of gray clouds in the sky, hunt for your raincoat. What you see are *stratus* (STRAT uhs) clouds. They are the lowest clouds in the sky. Stratus clouds are heavy with water. The rain that falls from these clouds is usually very light. But some stratus clouds, called *nimbostratus* (NIM boh STRAT uhs) clouds usually bring heavy thunderstorms or snow.

Cirrus Clouds

The highest clouds are called *cirrus* (SIHR uhs) clouds. They float where the air is very, very cold. The water that cirrus clouds are made of isn't in tiny drops. It's in the form of little ice crystals. The ice crystals make thin clouds that look like white feathers. Cirrus clouds in the sky mean fair weather.

Cumulus Clouds

Sometimes the sky is filled with clouds that look like balls of cotton. These beautiful, fluffy clouds are called *cumulus* (KYOO myoo luhs) clouds. They form higher in the sky than stratus clouds. You usually see them on fair days. But if they form on a hot, humid day, there might be some rain.

THINK ABOUT IT

What kind of weather might you expect if you see fluffy, white clouds on a cool day?

Precipitation

What is rain? Where does it come from? What does it have to do with clouds? Read on!

Even on a clear day, some water is in the air. But on some days, there is a lot of water in the air. As a cloud cools, more water drops form. They bump into each other and come together. This makes the drops heavy. Gravity pulls on them. The cloud can't hold the heavy drops anymore, and they fall to the ground. Water, either liquid or frozen, that falls from the sky to Earth is called *precipitation* (pree sip uh TAY shuhn).

You're very familiar with one kind of precipitation—rain. *Rain* is just water drops falling down from clouds.

▲ Sometimes the air around a cloud becomes very cold. The tiny drops of water in the cloud become frozen. They change into beautiful six-sided crystals of ice that fall to the ground. This kind of precipitation is *snow*.

Sometimes in the winter, drops of rain fall through a cold layer of air. The cold air turns the drops into small pieces of ice called *sleet*. Sleet is very slippery on the ground. It can cause dangerous conditions for driving on roads and even for walking on sidewalks. ▶

▲ Ice can form in clouds in the summer. If this ice mixes with drops of water in a cold part of the sky, the water freezes on the ice. This forms larger pieces of ice called *hail*. The hail starts to fall, but winds may blow it upward. Then another layer of water freezes over the hail. This can happen over and over. The hail can become as big as baseballs.

◀ Farmers fear hail. It can knock down crops such as corn and wheat and ruin them. Large hailstones can even damage the roofs of cars and houses.

THINK ABOUT IT

1. What are some problems that could be caused by the four different kinds of precipitation?

2. If you cut a hailstone in half, what kind of pattern do you think you would see? Draw what you might see.

3. During the summer of 1993, several states received so much rain that many streams and rivers flooded the land. What kinds of clouds probably were in the sky during this time?

Making a Rain Gauge

People who study weather measure the rainfall in different areas every month. They do this with a rain gauge. A rain gauge can also show how much water has fallen as snow, sleet, or hail. In this activity, you'll make a simple rain gauge.

DO THIS

1 Tape the ruler firmly to the container. The 1-cm-mark should be near the bottom of the container. The end near the 1 should be even with the bottom.

2 Place your rain gauge outside when rain is expected. Make sure the rain gauge is not under a tree or anything else.

3 When the rain has stopped, check the water level in the container. Record the rainfall in millimeters. Also record the date.

4 Empty your rain gauge. Then fill it about half full with ice cubes. These stand for large hailstones. Measure the height of the ice cubes in the rain gauge. Record the height.

MATERIALS
- clear plastic container (about 1 L or larger, with top cut off)
- ruler
- masking tape
- ice cubes
- Science Log data sheet

5 Let the ice melt. Then record the height of the water in the rain gauge.

6 Repeat steps 4 and 5 with snow, if you have it, instead of ice cubes.

7 Check the weather report for the day that you measured the rainfall. Find out how much rain fell. Compare the report with your data. Try to explain any difference.

THINK AND WRITE

1. Why do you think it's important to know how much rain an area usually gets?

2. Was the height of the ice cubes different from the height of the water after the ice cubes melted? What does this tell you about measuring the water that falls as hail?

3. Do you think 1 m of snowfall is the same as 1 m of rainfall? Why or why not?

4. **MEASURING** Suppose your rain gauge had been under a tree. Would your measurements have been different? Explain.

The Water Cycle

You've already learned that water vapor in the air condenses to form clouds. Water moves from clouds to the ground as precipitation. But how does the water get back into the air?

Water moves into the air from the ground and from bodies of water such as oceans and lakes. It becomes water vapor in the air through a process of *evaporation* (ee vap uh RAY shuhn). You've probably observed the results of evaporation after drying your hands on a towel. The towel becomes wet, but later it's dry again. The water has evaporated into the air.

The drawing on these pages shows the water cycle. The **water cycle** is the path that water follows as it moves from the air to the ground and back to the air over and over again. In the water cycle, water condenses, precipitates, and evaporates. It also travels over land, through rivers, and into the oceans. Follow the arrows to find out the path that water takes.

Most of the water in the air has evaporated from the oceans.

Water evaporates from streams and rivers. Some water in the soil evaporates into the air.

Rivers feed water into the oceans.

Streams feed water into rivers.

Water vapor in the air condenses to form clouds.

Precipitation falls from the clouds to the ground and into bodies of water.

When water falls on land, some soaks into the soil. Some flows over the land into streams.

QUICK CHECK

LESSON 4 REVIEW

1 How could looking at clouds help you predict the weather?

2 A terrarium is a tank that contains plants growing in soil. The soil is watered. Then the terrarium is completely sealed. Water cannot get in or out. How do the plants survive without being watered again?

3 You are indoors and hear thunder. You look outside and see heavy rain. What kind of cloud are you likely to see, and what does it look like?

DOUBLE CHECK

SECTION A REVIEW

1. What have you learned in this section that would help a weather forecaster predict the weather?

2. What would happen if rainwater did not evaporate back into the air?

Air Pressure

What is air? What might make you think it is nothing? What might make you think it is something?

Air looks like nothing. You can see right through it. However, you can also see through glass, and you know that glass is something. So being able to look through air isn't a good test to find out whether it is or is not something.

Have you ever bounced a basketball or played soccer? Have you ever lifted an air mattress out of a pool, or blown up an empty bag and popped it? What was in the things you were tossing, lifting, kicking, or popping? It was air.

In this section, you will learn some of the things we know about air. You will also learn how this information can help us understand how air and weather are related. Keep notes in your Science Log.

1 MORE ABOUT AIR

What would you think if you walked into your classroom and your teacher told you that you live in an "ocean"? What kind of ocean could the teacher be talking about? Sit very still and breathe deeply. What are you taking into your body? Perhaps air is the "ocean" the teacher means. In this lesson, you will discover something about air and why it is important to life on Earth.

What Is Matter?

Look around your classroom. What do you see? Name some of the objects.

In science, we say these things you are naming are all made of matter. **Matter** is anything that has mass and takes up space. What is mass? **Mass** is the amount of matter in an object.

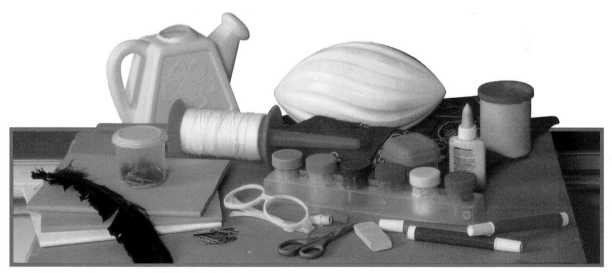

▲ All these things are made of matter.

THINK ABOUT IT

Are you made of matter? Explain why or why not.

How Much Matter?

Lift this book into the air. What do you feel? Does it feel heavy? You can find out how much mass the book has. Try this activity to find the mass of an object.

MATERIALS

- balance with gram masses
- large paper clips
- objects (eraser, pencil, paper clip, nickel)
- Science Log data sheet

DO THIS

❶ Copy the table shown here.

❷ Put one object on the right-hand pan of the balance.

❸ Put paper clips on the left-hand pan until the pointer is resting on zero.

❹ Record the name of the object and the number of paper clips it took to balance it.

❺ Repeat steps 2–4 with the other objects.

❻ Repeat steps 2–5. This time, use the gram masses provided with the balance.

HOW MUCH MASS?		
Object	Number of Paper Clips	Mass in Grams

THINK AND WRITE

1. List the objects in order from those with the least mass to those with the greatest mass. How did you know in what order to put the objects?

2. **MEASURING** People usually use an agreed-upon standard for measurements. In the activity, you measured the masses of several objects with paper clips and with gram masses. If you wanted to share your measurements of the masses of the objects with someone else, why would using paper clips not be the best idea?

Can You Weigh Air?

What happens when you throw a ball up into the air? Does it keep going up? Why or why not?

Earth's gravity pulls everything that has mass toward Earth's surface. Your ball comes down again, doesn't it? The measure of the pull of gravity on an object is called **weight.** If you lift a book, you can feel its weight pressing on your hand. If someone steps on your toes, you feel the weight on your foot.

We measure weight using a spring scale. Weight is measured in units called *newtons.*

Could you measure the weight of a scoop of air with a spring scale? Of course not! How would you attach the air to the spring scale? But that doesn't mean air doesn't have weight.

Think about a balloon. You know that when you blow up a balloon, it gets bigger because air takes up space inside the balloon. Anything that takes up space has mass. Because air has mass, gravity pulls on it. Therefore, we know that air has weight. The weight of the air presses on Earth's surface.

THINK ABOUT IT

How could you weigh the air in a balloon?

ACTIVITY

The Weight of Air

You may not be able to feel the air's weight. But, by doing this activity, you can observe that it does have weight.

DO THIS

1. Place the uninflated kickball in the mesh bag. Hang the bag from the hook of the spring scale. Read and record the number of newtons on the scale.

2. Repeat step 1, this time using the inflated kickball.

MATERIALS

- 2 identical kickballs, one inflated, one not inflated
- mesh bag
- spring scale
- Science Log data sheet

THINK AND WRITE

1. Did one ball weigh more than the other? How do you know?

2. How were the two balls different?

3. Does air have weight? How do you know?

Air Pressure

How do you erase a pencil mark? You press down on an eraser and move it back and forth, don't you? If you didn't put pressure on the eraser, it wouldn't clean off the pencil mark. Now you're going to study air pressure and why it's important.

160 km

Air presses on everything on Earth's surface. Even though you can't feel it, the weight of the air is pressing on you, too. The weight of air pressing on an area on Earth is called *air pressure*. In fact, a column of air about 160 kilometers (99 miles) high is pressing on you right now. This column of air, which weighs as much as a car, doesn't just press down on you. Since there is air all around you, it pushes against your body in all directions. The air has been pressing against you your entire life, which is why you don't notice it.

You use air pressure to do many things. For example, you use it when you drink through a straw. By sucking air from the straw into your mouth, you are removing air from inside the straw. Air pressure is pushing down on the liquid in the container. It pushes the liquid up the straw to replace the air you removed.

THINK ABOUT IT

How could you change the air pressure inside a bike tire?

Making a Barometer

In this activity, you can measure air pressure by building and using a barometer (buh RAHM uh tuhr).

DO THIS

1. Cut off the neck of the balloon. Stretch the bottom of the balloon over the top of the jar.

2. Fasten the balloon to the jar with a rubber band as shown. The balloon should be tight, like the head of a drum.

3. Tape one end of the straw to the center of the stretched balloon as shown.

4. **Caution: Be careful not to stick yourself with the pin.** Tape the pin to the other end of the straw.

5. Tape the bottom of the jar to the left side of the cardboard. The straw should be pointing to the right.

MATERIALS

- large balloon
- scissors
- wide-mouth jar
- rubber band
- transparent tape
- drinking straw
- pin
- corrugated cardboard
- index card
- ruler
- pencil
- Science Log data sheet

6 Draw lines across the unlined side of the index card every 0.5 cm from top to bottom. Number the lines from the bottom, starting with 1.

 7 Bend the bottom of the index card, and tape it to the cardboard. The number 1 should be at the bottom. The left edge of the index card should be alongside the pin but not touching it. Your setup should look like the one shown.

8 Observe the pin every 2 hours over the next 5 days. Record the position of the pin and the date and time of each observation.

THINK AND WRITE

1. What did the pin do as time passed?

2. Why do you think this happened?

3. How might you check to find out whether your idea is correct?

4. **INTERPRETING DATA** When you make measurements, you collect data, or information. What you do next is very important. You try to figure out what the data means. What do you think the data means in the activity you just did?

The Development of Barometers

Barometers have led to many discoveries about the air. With a barometer, you can see how air pressure changes as you climb a mountain. You already know that a barometer measures air pressure. Barometers are also used to predict weather. This time line shows when different barometers were developed and how they added to our knowledge.

1640

1643

In 1643, Italian scientist Evangelista Torricelli (eh vahn jeh LEES tah • tawr uh CHEL ee) invented the first barometer. It was a very simple instrument. Torricelli's barometer was nothing more than a long glass tube filled with mercury. The tube sat in a cup that was also filled with mercury. When Torricelli put the tube in the cup, the mercury began running out the bottom of the tube into the cup. Suddenly, the mercury stopped running out. A column of mercury 76 centimeters (30 inches) tall stayed in the tube. What was pushing the mercury up?

1648

In 1648, French scientist Blaise Pascal performed an investigation. He gave his brother-in-law, Florin Perier (FLOHR ihn • peh ree AY), a barometer. Pascal then sent Perier up a mountain 1,460 meters (4,790 feet) tall. As Perier climbed up, the column of mercury in the barometer became shorter and shorter. At the top of the mountain, the column was about 7 centimeters (3 inches) shorter than it had been at the bottom. The only way to explain this observation was that on top of the mountain, less air was pressing down on the barometer.

1652

In 1652, German scientist Otto von Guericke (GEHR ik uh) used a barometer to predict the coming of a storm. This was the first time a barometer had been used to make a weather prediction. Guericke had heard that air pressure went down before a storm. So he watched his barometer carefully. When he saw that the air pressure was dropping, he predicted that a storm would occur. Unfortunately, Guericke's barometer broke. But the storm came anyway.

Altimeter ▶

Today

Today, people use barometers called *aneroid* (AN uh royd) *barometers*. They work very much like the balloon barometer you made in the activity Making a Barometer. As air pressure changes, a needle on the face of the barometer moves. The barometer has numbers on it that show the air pressure. You would find a barometer like this in homes, offices and schools. Some are shaped like clocks.

As Pascal discovered, air pressure changes as you go higher. The higher you are, the less air there is above you. So there is less of it pressing down on you. Air pressure is lower at the top of a mountain than it is in a valley.

Airplane pilots use a type of barometer called an altimeter (al TIM uht uhr). An altimeter measures the changes in pressure that occur when an airplane goes higher or lower in its flight. By reading the altimeter, a pilot can help keep the plane at the right height to be safe.

QUICK CHECK

LESSON 1 REVIEW

How would the measurements of a barometer you are holding change in the following situations? Give a reason for your answer.

a. You ride on an elevator from the twentieth floor to the first floor.

b. You climb a hill.

c. You walk across the schoolyard.

2 PREDICTING WEATHER

Barometers can be used to predict the weather. A drop in pressure, shown when the needle points to a lower number, often means that stormy weather is coming. An increase in pressure, shown when the needle points to a higher number, usually means that fair weather is on the way.

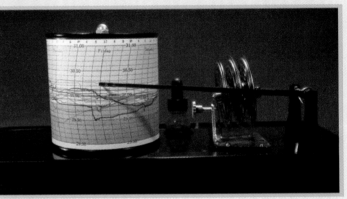

ACTIVITY

Air Pressure and Weather Prediction

Weather forecasters use barometers to help them predict the weather. To see how, try this activity.

MATERIALS
- barometer made in the activity on pages B46–B47.
- Science Log data sheet

DO THIS

① Draw a chart like the one below.

WEATHER OBSERVATIONS		
Date	Barometer Reading	Weather

2 For 5 days in a row, at the same time each day, measure and record the barometer reading. Beside your readings, write down what the weather is like.

3 After taking the reading on the fifth day, make a prediction about the kind of weather you think is coming in 2 days.

4 On the second day after you make your prediction, watch the weather report on the evening news or find it in the newspaper the next day. Record the day's actual weather. Also, record any unusual or sudden change in weather conditions mentioned by the weatherperson.

THINK AND WRITE

1. Why did you make the prediction that you did?

2. Was your prediction correct? Explain why or why not.

Changes in Air Pressure

You now know that a change in air pressure usually means a change in weather. But what does a change in air pressure have to do with the weather?

High in the sky, the air is very cold. Cool air is heavier than warm air, so the heavy, cold air sinks to the ground. The sinking cold air pushes under the warmer air near Earth's surface. This forces the warm air upward.

As cool air moves downward, it presses more on Earth's surface. As a result, the air pressure there is higher. As warm air moves upward, it presses less on the surface. So air pressure there is lower.

You may remember from the last section that warm air can hold more moisture than cold air. Areas of low pressure often have cloudy weather and rain or snow. Areas where there is high pressure usually have fair weather.

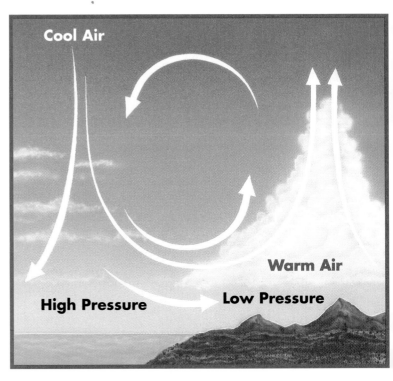

Cool Air

Warm Air

High Pressure → Low Pressure

THINK ABOUT IT

Look at the pictures. Is the air pressure low or high in each scene? How do you know?

Bill Beams
He Collects Weather Data

Next time you are warned of a coming storm, you might have Bill Beams to thank. That's because Beams leads a team of scientists at the National Weather Service in Amarillo, Texas.

The team's job is to gather data from the sky. The team gets data on weather conditions in different ways.

Some data comes from using radar. Radar bounces radio signals off objects. The signals come back like echoes. The scientists use the radar to find clouds, rain, and snow in the sky. By studying the echoes, they can tell which way clouds and weather are moving.

Bill Beams ▼

The information from the radar is shown with a map on a computer screen. ▼

Some data comes from balloons that float high into the air. The balloons collect data on such things as temperature and air pressure.

The data collected by the team is sent to Camp Springs, Maryland. So is data from teams at other weather stations all over the country. Weather scientists in Camp Springs interpret the data from everywhere and then provide this information to weather forecasters across the country.

Besides his job, Beams has many other interests. He is very involved in the cultural life of his people, the Choctaw.

Beams launching a weather balloon ▶

Beams has also visited many schools to talk to students about the weather. He tells students that if they are interested in becoming weather scientists, they should read a lot about the weather. They should also study lots of math and science.

Beams talking to students about weather ▼

QUICK CHECK

LESSON 2 REVIEW

❶ What instruments do weather scientists use to gather the data they use to predict the weather? What kind of information does each instrument provide?

❷ After three days of fair weather, there is a rainy day. What would you expect your barometer to show over the four days?

✓ DOUBLE CHECK

SECTION B REVIEW

1. What is air pressure? How can it be measured?

2. Why is it useful to measure air pressure?

3. Why do you think weather scientists gather data from all across the country?

SECTION C
Air Pollution

If you listen to a weather report on television or radio, you'll find out how warm or cold it will probably be. And you'll learn if rain or snow is expected. But you can also find out about something else. You can find out how clean or dirty the air is. This condition of the air is called *air quality.*

The air quality depends on how much pollution is in the air. It also has something to do with the weather. How are air pollution and weather related? Why can you find information on air pollution in the weather report? Why would you want to know this information?

In this section, you'll find out how weather and air quality are related. You'll also find out why this information is important. Keep notes in your Science Log.

1 WHAT IS AIR POLLUTION?

If you live in or near a city, you see many cars and trucks. You may also have smelled an odor given off from their exhaust pipes. You have seen smoke from factories or burning garbage. Even away from the city, you can see smoke from fireplaces or notice odors in the air. All of these things can be a sign of air pollution. What types of things cause air pollution? Can air pollution be identified or measured? You are about to investigate these questions.

What Causes Air Pollution?

About 15 times every minute, you do something that keeps you alive. Stop for a moment and think what this "something" might be.

The "something" that you do is breathe. In that minute, you take in enough air to fill almost three large (two-liter) soft-drink bottles. In a day, you breathe in enough air to fill a box the size of a small house. Part of that air is a gas called *oxygen.* You need oxygen to stay alive. So do other animals and plants.

But sometimes the air holds materials that are harmful to plants and animals. These materials are called *air pollution.* Air pollution can be solid particles or gases. What are these things that don't belong in the air? Where do they come from?

▲ When cars, trucks, and buses burn fuel, they give off exhaust. In the exhaust are gases and particles of liquids or solids that go into the air. Sometimes you can see the exhaust coming out of tailpipes.

Energy plants give us electricity. We need electricity for our homes, businesses, and factories. But some energy plants burn fuels such as coal or oil to generate electricity. The burning fuels release gases and solids into the air.

Some factories also add to air pollution. These factories use a lot of chemicals or metals to make things. Gases and tiny bits of metal are sent into the air through the factories' smokestacks. ▶

◀ Not all air pollution is caused by people. Some is caused by natural events, such as forest fires and the eruption of volcanoes. The smoke and dust particles in the air make it hard for people and animals to breathe.

THINK ABOUT IT

What are some ways people could reduce air pollution?

Making Soot

Soot is made of tiny, solid particles that get into the air. Little pieces of soot can make your skin and clothes dirty. Soot can get into your lungs when you breathe. Where does soot come from? Try this activity to see if you can find out.

DO THIS

1. Your teacher will light one candle and place it on a heat-proof pad. Place the other candle nearby, but do not light it.

2. Look above both candles. Describe what, if anything, you see.

3. Next, use the thermal mitt to hold one aluminum pan a few centimeters over the burning candle. **CAUTION: Keep your fingers away from the flame.** After a few seconds, take the pan away. Your teacher will blow out the candle.

4. Hold the other pan for a few seconds over the candle that is not burning.

5. Look at the part of each pan that was over a candle. Record what you see.

THINK AND WRITE

1. What process produces soot? How did you reach this conclusion?

2. Think about what you saw above the burning candle. Where would the soot you gathered on the bottom of the pan have gone if the pan hadn't been there?

3. Name two other things that might produce soot.

ACTIVITY

Can You See Air Pollution?

Scientists have many instruments they use to tell how much pollution is in the air. However, you don't need complex instruments to measure certain kinds of air pollution. This activity will give you a way to find out how much pollution is in the air.

DO THIS

1 Make a chart like the one shown.

AIR POLLUTION		
Slide Number	Location	Description of Slide After One Week
1		
2		
3		
4		

2 Use the wax pencil to number the four slides 1, 2, 3, and 4.

3 Cover half of each slide with a thin coat of petroleum jelly.

4 Put 3 of the slides (with the jelly side up) in different places. At least one should be outdoors. Make sure the slides won't be disturbed for a week. Write the location of each slide on your chart.

5 Put the fourth slide (with its jelly side up) in the box. Put the lid on the box. Place the box in a safe spot in the classroom.

6 After a week, gather the slides. Hold them up to the light and examine them with a hand lens. In your chart, describe what you see on each slide.

THINK AND WRITE

1. What difference, if any, did you find between the slide from inside the box and the other slides?

2. How might people be affected by breathing polluted air?

3. COMMUNICATING Communicating the results of an investigation is important. What data did you collect in this investigation? How did you communicate what you found?

Air Temperature and Pollution

Does air temperature affect pollution? If it does, how does it affect pollution? Read on!

Pollution is usually carried high into the air, away from its source. But air pollution near the ground can be made worse by certain weather conditions.

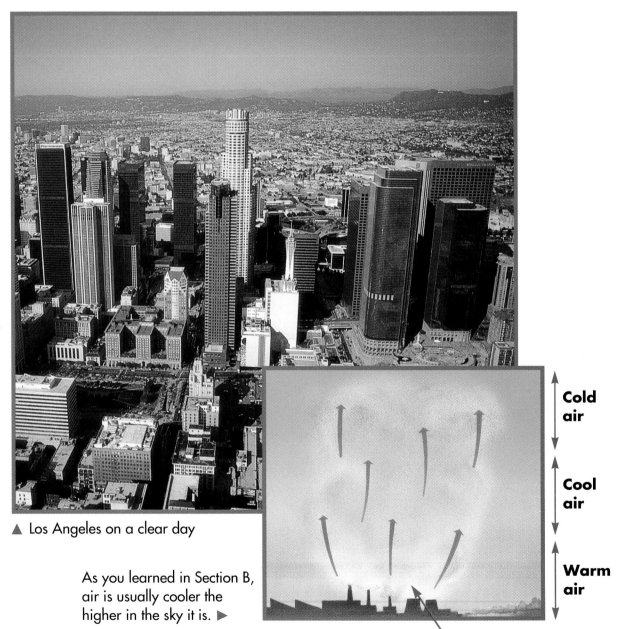

▲ Los Angeles on a clear day

As you learned in Section B, air is usually cooler the higher in the sky it is. ▶

Cold air

Cool air

Warm air

Polluted air

Los Angeles when pollution is "trapped" ▼

Cold, clean air

Warm air

Cool, polluted air

◀ Sometimes a layer of warm air moves in over cooler air that is near the ground. Then you have a sandwich of warm air between a cooler layer below and a much colder layer above. The layer of much colder air above the warm air keeps the warm air from being pushed upward. Therefore, the warm air layer traps the cooler air near the ground. The pollution in the cooler air is also trapped near the ground.

QUICK CHECK

LESSON 1 REVIEW

Why might weather scientists measure the amount of pollution in the air?

2 AIR POLLUTION AND YOU

If you live in some of the northern parts of the United States, you can usually expect a lot of snow in the winter. Some days, there may be so much snow on the roads that school is canceled. You might even enjoy the extra time off to play in the snow with your friends.

But what if school were canceled because too much pollution was in the air? That's just what happened in Mexico City, Mexico. School had to be canceled for an entire month in January of 1989. The air was so badly polluted that the children could not go outside.

▲ Breathing the air in Mexico City can be as bad for your lungs as smoking two packs of cigarettes a day.

Air Pollution and Your Health

You have already learned that polluted air has tiny particles and certain gases in it. These particles and gases are called *pollutants*, and they harm people and other living things. In people, air pollution does the most harm to the lungs and the heart. Over a long time, air pollution can increase a person's chances of getting lung disease or heart disease.

Air pollution hurts some people more than others. The groups hit the hardest include very old and very young people. Their lungs are especially sensitive to polluted air. People who already

▲ Why is this cyclist wearing a mask?

have diseases that affect their lungs or heart are also harmed more than other people are by air pollution.

Exhaust from cars, trucks, and buses cause up to half of all the pollution in many cities. The exhaust irritates people's eyes. It also gets into people's lungs.

Your body needs oxygen to live. One kind of gas in exhausts moves from the lungs into the blood. It takes up the place in the blood where oxygen is held. So the gas keeps the body from getting enough oxygen.

Other gases that form when fuel is burned are also harmful if you inhale them. One of these gases can kill your lung cells. It can also cause fluid to build up in your lungs. This makes it harder to breathe and can cause lung disease.

Another gas made when fuel is burned is ozone (OH zohn). If you breathe ozone, it makes you cough and hurts your throat. It also keeps you from getting enough oxygen into your body. Breathing ozone in polluted air can worsen the lung diseases and heart diseases people already have.

You read earlier that some factories send tiny bits of metal into the air. Tiny bits of a metal called *lead* are very harmful when inhaled. The inhaled lead builds up in bones, kidneys, and the brain.

Lead is especially harmful to infants and children. It can harm all the parts inside the body. Lead's most serious effect is brain damage. Even small amounts of lead can affect how you are able to learn, to remember things, and to concentrate.

THINK ABOUT IT

How is air pollution dangerous to you?

ACTIVITY

The Effects of Acid Rain

Certain gases from factories and energy plants turn rain into a weak acid similar to vinegar. When this acid rain falls on trees, it can injure or kill them. Acid rain also wears away stone statues and buildings. In the following activity, you will make a model of acid rain and investigate its effects.

MATERIALS

- safety goggles
- 2 clear plastic cups
- vinegar (100 mL)
- distilled water (100 mL)
- 2 pieces of chalk
- pencil
- Science Log data sheet

DO THIS

❶ CAUTION: Wear safety goggles during this activity. Label one cup *Vinegar* and the other cup *Water*.

❷ Fill the cup labeled *Vinegar* one-third full with vinegar. Fill the other cup one-third full with distilled water.

❸ Drop one piece of chalk into the vinegar and one into the water.

❹ Watch both pieces of chalk for a few minutes. Record what you observe.

❺ With the pencil, poke at the chalk in each cup. Record how each piece of chalk feels.

THINK AND WRITE

1. What did the vinegar stand for in this activity?

2. What can you infer about acid rain's effect on stone from your observations? Explain why.

Acid Rain and How It Forms

One way to learn more about acid rain is to read about it. These pages tell you how acid rain harms animals, plants, and even stone. You will learn where the acid comes from and how it gets into the rain. You will also find out what is being done to prevent acid rain. As you read, think about any effects of acid rain you may have seen.

Can Rain Be Dangerous?

from *Current Health 1*

 LITERATURE "What does it take for plants to grow?" Mr. West asked at the beginning of science class.

Several hands went up. The answers included "Sunshine!" "Good soil!" "Fertilizer!" "Rain!"

All of the answers were correct, but then Mr. West told the students in his class something they didn't know—that rain can sometimes kill plants.

"That happens when the rain falls through the dirty air," Mr. West explained. "The rain itself then becomes dirty and full of chemicals, especially acids, that can kill forests and plants and even poison the water of lakes and streams. This kind of rain is called acid rain," Mr. West said. "It can also be sleet, snow, fog, or even dust."

▲ Pollution has been a problem for more than 100 years.

Mr. West explained that people first learned about acid rain more than 100 years ago when a scientist tested rain that had fallen in cities in England, Scotland, and Germany. He found that the rain was full of acid. He also learned that the acid in the rain was caused by pollution trapped in the air.

"Did they have pollution even back then?" Bobby asked.

"Oh, yes," Mr. West said, "because there were factories then, too, with smokestacks just as we have today. Also, people burned coal and oil for heat and that caused pollution. Burning coal and oil fills the air with a chemical called sulfur dioxide. When sulfur dioxide mixes with moisture in the air, a chemical called sulfuric acid is formed. Other gases from cars and the factories mixed with moisture to form nitric acid. Even today, many factories, energy plants, and cars still release these chemicals."

Mr. West saw the puzzled look on

Chuck's face and the way his hand came up slowly. "Did you have a question, Chuck?" he asked.

"It's not a question exactly," Chuck said. "It's just that there is something I don't understand. My grandparents live near a forest in Vermont, and that forest has got a lot of dead trees in it. My grandpa says acid rain killed them. But there are no factories nearby. There are just some small towns and lots of countryside. So how could it be acid rain that killed the forest?"

"That's a good question, Chuck," Mr. West said. "There doesn't have to be a factory nearby for acid rain to fall. You see, when the chemicals mix with the moisture, they form acid pollution that moves across the sky on air currents (bodies of air that always move in a certain direction). Most of the time, air currents in the United States move from west to east. There are a lot of factories and energy plants in the Ohio Valley. Pollution from those factories and plants often travels hundreds of miles, even as far as Vermont or Canada,

before it falls to the ground in the form of acid rain and affects lakes and forests."

"But I thought there were laws against factories causing pollution," Chuck said.

"You're right, there are," Mr. West said. "But some of the first laws that were passed didn't help much. One of those early laws said that smokestacks on factories had to be taller. That meant the pollutants were pushed higher into the air. That helped clean up the air in the cities where the factories were located, but it also pushed the pollutants up where wind currents could carry them somewhere else."

▲ Trees all over the world, like these in the Great Smoky Mountains, have been damaged by acid rain.

▲ A chemical called lime can stop a lake from getting too high in acid content. Airplanes are used to drop lime into the lakes.

Problems Needing Solutions

Another problem, Mr. West explained, is that changes to factories that produce pollution cost a lot of money. Besides, since no one has figured out exactly *how* acid rain kills trees, some people say that means there is no proof that it is acid rain that is killing them.

"However, not all factory and energy plant owners feel that way," Mr. West said. "Some even have experts study acid rain and how to control it."

Fish Are in Danger, Too

"Forests aren't the only things in danger. Acid rain also makes lakes polluted," Mr. West continued. "Some lakes get so much acid in them from the rain that fish cannot live in them."

Besides the damage done to water and forests, acid rain can also harm buildings. It can cause them to wear away or to become full of cracks or holes.

A Quick Solution?

"Can things get worse if acid rain keeps falling?" asked Robin.

"Yes, I think things *can* get worse," Mr. West said. "Recently, we have had a chance to see just how bad things can be when there are no controls on the pollution that causes acid rain. In Poland there were very few laws against pollution for a long time. Now, in some parts of that country, there is barren land where there were once forests."

Acid rain can wear away the stone of buildings and statues. ▶

"How can we keep that from happening here?" Anne asked.

"Some people say we need to study the problem some more to find out exactly how acid rain causes damage. Others say we can't wait. They say we have to make the rules for factories and energy plants even stricter so fewer chemicals are released into the air. They say we should use less electricity so energy plants won't have to burn so much coal. They also say we need to find other fuels to use besides coal and oil and gasoline for cars, so the air is not so dirty."

Mr. West's class decided to vote on whether more study should be done on acid rain first, and if enough is being done about pollution now. How do you think the vote came out? How would *your* class vote?

▲ The smoke from this energy plant is made by burning coal.

DOUBLE CHECK

SECTION C REVIEW

1. Weather reporters often mention the air quality to let people know the amount of pollution in the air. Why might people want this information?

2. What might happen if more and more pollution were released into the air? Why is it a good idea to reduce pollution as much as possible?

I REFLECT

It's time to think about the ideas you have discovered during your investigations. Think, too, about your many accomplishments.

SUMMARIZE

Answer the following in your Science Log.

1. What **I Wonder** questions have you answered in your investigations? What new questions have you asked?

2. What have you discovered about air and weather? How have your ideas changed?

3. Did any of your discoveries surprise you? Explain.

CONNECT IDEAS

1. Suppose you wanted to make your own weather station. Tell what you would include in your station and why.

2. Write a paragraph or draw a diagram to explain why there are seasons.

3. When you exercise, you need to breathe in a lot more oxygen than when you're resting. Why would it be harmful to exercise when the air is polluted with ozone?

4. Draw four diagrams. Draw one for each of the four kinds of precipitation. On your diagrams, label each step in the process that forms the precipitation.

5. What kinds of things are people doing to make sure we have clean air to breathe?

SCIENCE PORTFOLIO

❶ Complete your Science Experiences Record.

❷ Choose one or two samples of your best work from each section to include in your Science Portfolio.

❸ On A Guide to My Science Portfolio, tell why you chose each sample.

I SHARE

Scientists share their discoveries and ideas and learn from one another. How can you share what you've learned?

Decide

► what you want to say.

► what the best way is to get your message across.

Share

► what you did and why.

► what worked and what didn't work.

► what conclusions you have drawn.

► what else you'd like to find out.

Find Out

► what classmates liked about what you shared—and why.

► what questions your classmates have.

I ACT

Science is more than discoveries—it is also what you do with those discoveries. How might you use what you have learned about the air and weather?

▶ Read newspapers and listen to news reports to find out about air pollution where you live. Make a list of things you and your classmates can do to help make the air cleaner.

▶ Set up a weather station at your school. Collect data and predict the weather. Show the weather instruments to other classes, and explain how to use them.

▶ Keep a weather log for 30 days. Write a newsletter describing your findings.

▶ Find a new way to enjoy a sunny day, a windy day, a rainy day, or a snowy day.

THE LANGUAGE OF SCIENCE

The language of science helps people communicate clearly when they talk about nature. Here are some vocabulary words you can use when you talk about air and weather with friends, family, and others.

air pollution—solid particles or gases that do not belong in the air and that are harmful to organisms. Air pollution is caused by car exhausts, burning fuels, burning trash, factories, forest fires, and erupting volcanoes. **(B59)**

air pressure—the weight of air pressing on an area of Earth's surface. Dropping air pressure means that precipitation is coming. Rising air pressure means that fair weather is coming. **(B45)**

axis—an imaginary line that runs from Earth's North Pole to its South Pole. Earth is tilted on its axis. **(B19)**

barometer—an instrument that measures air pressure. Aneroid barometers have a dial and a needle. The needle points to a place on the dial to show the air pressure. Mercury barometers use mercury in a sealed tube to measure air pressure. **(B46)**

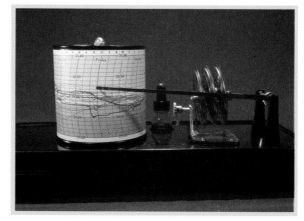

▲ Barometer

cirrus clouds—the highest clouds in the sky. They are thin and signal fair weather. **(B33)**

▲ Cirrus clouds

condensation—the process by which a gas changes to a liquid. Water droplets form when water vapor becomes liquid water. **(B27)**

▲ This pitcher has condensation on it.

cumulus clouds—fluffy clouds that usually signal fair weather but may bring rain or snow. **(B33)**

dew—water vapor that condenses on surfaces in cool morning air. Dew forms when the temperature of moist air falls to a certain level. **(B28)**

equator—an imaginary line that runs around Earth and splits it into a northern half and a southern half. **(B19)**

evaporation—the process by which liquid water turns into water vapor. Liquid water returns to the air through evaporation. **(B38)**

humidity—the amount of water vapor in the air. **(B27)**

mass—the amount of matter in an object. You use a balance to find the mass of an object. **(B41)**

matter—anything that has mass and takes up space. All objects are made of matter. **(B41)**

nimbostratus clouds—stratus clouds that are very dark and thick. These clouds bring heavy rain or snow and thunder and lightning. **(B32)**

▲ Cumulus clouds

Nimbostratus clouds ▶

precipitation—water, either liquid or frozen, that falls from the clouds. Four kinds of precipitation are rain, snow, sleet, and hail. **(B34)**

stratus clouds—low, thick clouds that usually bring rain. **(B32)**

Snow is one type of precipitation. ▼

▲ Stratus clouds

thermometer—an instrument used to measure temperatures. **(B14)**

water cycle—the movement of water from place to place between Earth and the air. The water cycle includes the processes of evaporation and condensation. **(B38)**

water vapor—water in the form of a gas. **(B27)**

weight—the measure of the pull of gravity on matter. **(B43)**

Water cycle ▼

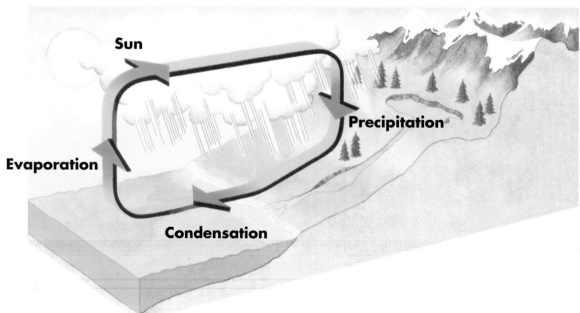

Sun

Precipitation

Evaporation

Condensation

REFERENCE HANDBOOK

Safety in the Classroom

Doing activities in science can be fun, but you need to be sure you do them safely. It is up to you, your teacher, and your classmates to make your classroom a safe place for science activities.

Think about what causes most accidents in everyday life—being careless, not paying attention, and showing off. The same kinds of behavior cause accidents in the science classroom.

Here are some ways to make your classroom a safe place.

THINK AHEAD.

Study the steps of the activity so you know what to expect. If you have any questions about the steps, ask your teacher to explain. Be sure you understand any safety symbols that are shown in the activity.

WATCH YOUR EYES.

Wear safety goggles anytime you are directed to do so. If you should ever get any substance in your eyes, tell your teacher right away.

BE NEAT.

Keep your work area clean. If you have long hair, pull it back so it doesn't get in the way. If you have long sleeves, roll them or push them up to keep them away from your experiment.

OOPS!

If you should have an accident that causes a spill or breaks something, or if you get cut, tell your teacher right away.

YUCK!

Never eat or drink anything during a science activity unless you are told to do so by your teacher.

KEEP IT CLEAN.

Always clean up when you have finished your activity. Put everything away and wipe your work area. Last of all, wash your hands.

DON'T GET SHOCKED.

Sometimes you need to use electric appliances, such as lamps, in an activity. You always need to be careful around electricity. Be sure that electric cords are in a safe place where you can't trip over them. Don't ever pull a plug out of an outlet by pulling on the cord.

Safety Symbols

In some activities, you will see a symbol that stands for what you need to do to stay safe. Do what the symbol stands for.

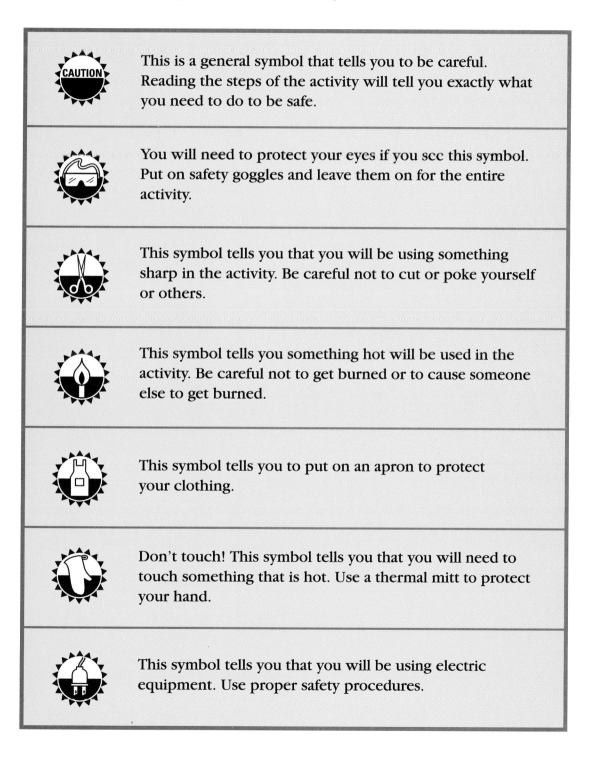

This is a general symbol that tells you to be careful. Reading the steps of the activity will tell you exactly what you need to do to be safe.

You will need to protect your eyes if you see this symbol. Put on safety goggles and leave them on for the entire activity.

This symbol tells you that you will be using something sharp in the activity. Be careful not to cut or poke yourself or others.

This symbol tells you something hot will be used in the activity. Be careful not to get burned or to cause someone else to get burned.

This symbol tells you to put on an apron to protect your clothing.

Don't touch! This symbol tells you that you will need to touch something that is hot. Use a thermal mitt to protect your hand.

This symbol tells you that you will be using electric equipment. Use proper safety procedures.

Using a Hand Lens

A hand lens magnifies objects, or makes them look larger than they are.

▲ **This object is not in focus.**

Sometimes objects are too small for you to see easily without some help. You might want to see details that you cannot see with your eyes alone. When this happens, you can use a hand lens.

To use a hand lens, first place the object you want to look at on a flat surface, such as a table. Next, hold the hand lens over the object. At first, the object may appear blurry, like the object in **A**. Move the hand lens toward or away from the object until the object comes into sharp focus, as shown in **B**.

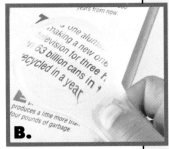

▲ **This object is focused clearly.**

Making a Water-Drop Lens

There may be times when you want to use a hand lens but there isn't one around. If that happens, you can make a water-drop lens to help you in the same way a hand lens does. A water-drop lens is best used to make flat objects, such as pieces of paper and leaves, seem larger.

MATERIALS
- sheet of acetate
- 2 rectangular rubber erasers
- water
- dropper

DO THIS

 Place the object to be magnified on a table between two identical erasers.

 Place a sheet of acetate on top of the erasers so that the sheet of acetate is about 1 cm above the object.

❸ Use the dropper to place one drop of water on the surface of the sheet over the object. Don't make the drop too large or it will make things look bent.

A water-drop lens can magnify objects. ▶

Caring For and Using a Microscope

A microscope, like a hand lens, magnifies objects. However, a microscope can increase the detail you see by increasing the number of times an object is magnified.

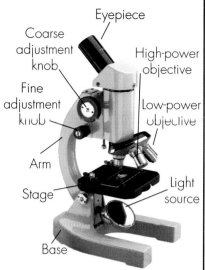

▲ **Light microscope**

CARING FOR A MICROSCOPE

- Always use two hands when you carry a microscope.
- Never touch any of the lenses of the microscope with your fingers.

USING A MICROSCOPE

1 Raise the eyepiece as far as you can using the coarse-adjustment knob. Place the slide you wish to view on the stage.

2 Always start by using the lowest power. The lowest-power lens is usually the shortest. Start with the lens in the lowest position it can go without touching the slide.

3 Look through the eyepiece and begin adjusting the eyepiece upward with the coarse-adjustment knob. When the slide is close to being in focus, use the fine-adjustment knob.

4 When you want to use the higher-power lens, first focus the slide under low power. Then, watching carefully to make sure that the lens will not hit the slide, turn the higher-power lens into place. Use only the fine-adjustment knob when looking through the higher-power lens.

Some of you may use a Brock microscope. This is a sturdy microscope that has only one lens.

1 Place the object to be viewed on the stage. Move the long tube, containing the lens, close to the stage.

2 Put your eye on the eyepiece, and begin raising the tube until the object comes into focus.

▲ **Brock microscope**

Using a Dropper

Use a dropper when you need to add small amounts of a liquid to another material.

A dropper has two main parts. One is a large empty part called a *bulb*. You hold the bulb and squeeze it to use the dropper. The other part of a dropper is long and narrow and is called a *tube*.

DO THIS

 Use a clean dropper for each liquid you measure.

2 With the dropper out of the liquid, squeeze the bulb and keep it squeezed. Then dip the end of the tube into the liquid.

3 Release the pressure on the bulb. As you do so, you will see the liquid enter the tube.

▲ **Using a dropper correctly**

4 Take the dropper from the liquid, and move it to the place you want to put the liquid. If you are putting the liquid into another liquid, do not let the dropper touch the surface of the second liquid.

5 Gently squeeze the bulb until one drop comes out of the tube. Repeat slowly until you have measured out the right number of drops.

▲ **Using a dropper incorrectly**

Measuring Liquids

Use a beaker, a measuring cup, or a graduated cylinder to measure liquids accurately.

Containers for measuring liquids are made of clear or translucent materials so that you can see the liquid inside them. On the outside of each of these measuring tools, you will see lines and numbers that make up a scale. On most of the containers used by scientists, the scale is in milliliters (mL).

DO THIS

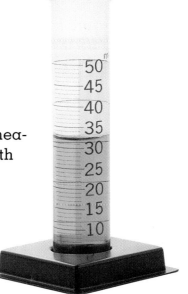

1. Pour the liquid you want to measure into one of the measuring containers. Make sure your measuring container is on a flat, stable surface, with the measuring scale facing you.

2. Look at the liquid through the container. Move so that your eyes are even with the surface of the liquid in the container.

3. To read the volume of the liquid, find the scale line that is even with the top of the liquid. In narrow containers, the surface of the liquid may look curved. Take your reading at the lowest point of the curve.

▲ There are 32 mL of liquid in this graduated cylinder.

4. Sometimes the surface of the liquid may not be exactly even with a line. In that case, you will need to estimate the volume of the liquid. Decide which line the liquid is closer to, and use that number.

▲ There are 27 mL of liquid in this beaker.

Using a Thermometer

Determine temperature readings of the air and most liquids by using a thermometer with a standard scale.

Most thermometers are thin tubes of glass that are filled with a red or silver liquid. As the temperature goes up, the liquid in the tube rises. As the temperature goes down, the liquid sinks. The tube is marked with lines and numbers that provide a temperature scale in degrees. Scientists use the Celsius scale to measure temperature. A temperature reading of 27 degrees Celsius is written 27°C.

DO THIS

❶ Place the thermometer in the liquid whose temperature you want to record, but don't rest the bulb of the thermometer on the bottom or side of the container. If you are measuring the temperature of the air, make sure that the thermometer is not in direct sunlight or in line with a direct light source.

❷ Move so that your eyes are e the liquid in the thermomete

❸ If you are measuring a material that is not being heated or cooled, wait about two minutes for the reading to become stable. Find the scale line that meet the top of the liquid in the thermometer, and read the temperature.

❹ If the material you are measuring is being heated o cooled, you will not be able t wait before taking your measurements. Measure as quickly as you can.

The temperature of this liquid is 27°C. ▶

Making a Thermometer

If you don't have a thermometer, you can make a simple one easily. The simple thermometer won't give you an exact temperature reading, but you can use it to tell if the temperature is going up or going down.

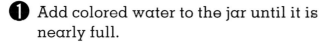

MATERIALS
- small, narrow-mouthed jar
- colored water
- clear plastic straw
- ruler
- clay
- dropper
- pen, pencil, or marker
- bowl of ice
- bowl of warm water

DO THIS

1 Add colored water to the jar until it is nearly full.

2 Place the straw in the jar. Finish filling the jar with water, but leave about 1 cm of space at the top.

3 Lift the straw until 10 cm of it stick up out of the jar. Use the clay to seal the mouth of the jar.

4 Use the dropper to add colored water to the straw until the straw is at least half full.

5 On the straw, mark the level of the water. "S" stands for *start*.

6 To get an idea of how your thermometer works, place the jar in a bowl of ice. Wait several minutes, and then mark the new water level on the straw. This new water level should be marked C for *cold*.

7 Take the jar out of the bowl of ice, and let it return to room temperature. Next, place the jar in a bowl of warm water. Wait several minutes, and then mark the new water level on the straw. This level can be labeled W for *warm*.

▶ You can use a thermometer like this to decide if the temperature of a liquid or the air is going up or down.

Using a Balance

Use a balance to measure an object's mass. Mass is the amount of matter an object has.

Most balances look like the one shown. They have two pans. In one pan, you place the object you want to measure. In the other pan, you place standard masses. Standard masses are objects that have a known mass. Grams are the units used to measure mass for most scientific activities.

DO THIS

 First, make certain the empty pans are balanced. They are in balance if the pointer is at the middle mark on the base. If the pointer is not at this mark, move the slider to the right or left. Your teacher will help if you cannot balance the pans.

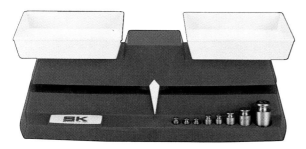

◀ **These pans are balanced and ready to be used to find the mass of an object.**

❷ Place the object you wish to measure in one pan. The pointer will move toward the pan without the object in it.

❸ Add the standard masses to the other pan. As you add masses, you should see the pointer begin to move. When the pointer is at the middle mark again, the pans are balanced.

❹ Add the numbers on the masses you used. The total is the mass of the object you measured.

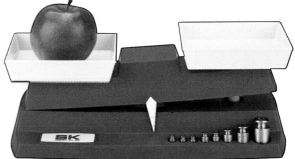

These pans are unbalanced. ▶

Making a Balance

If you do not have a balance, you can make one. A balance requires only a few simple materials. You can use nonstandard masses such as paper clips or nickels. This type of balance is best for measuring small masses.

DO THIS

MATERIALS
- 1 sturdy plastic or wooden ruler
- string
- transparent tape
- 2 paper cups
- 2 large paper clips

❶ If the ruler has holes in it, tie the string through the center hole. If it does not have holes, tie the string around the middle of the ruler.

❷ Tape the other end of the string to a table. Allow the ruler to hang down from the side of the table. Adjust the ruler so that it is level.

❸ Unbend the end of each paper clip slightly. Push these ends through the paper cups as shown. Attach each cup to the ruler by using the paper clips.

❹ Adjust the cups until the ruler is level again.

▶ **This balance is ready for use.**

Using a Spring Scale

A spring scale is a tool you use to measure the force of gravity on objects. You find the weight of the objects and use newtons as the unit of measurement for the force of gravity. You also use the spring scale and newtons to measure other forces.

A spring scale has two main parts. One part is a spring with a hook on the end. The hook is used to connect an object to the spring scale. The other part is a scale with numbers that tell you how many newtons of force are acting on the object.

DO THIS

With an Object at Rest

> With the object resting on the table, hook the spring scale to it. Do not stretch the spring at this point.
>
> Lift the scale and object with a smooth motion. Do not jerk them upward.
>
> Wait until any motion in the spring comes to a stop. Then read the number of newtons from the scale.

With an Object in Motion

> With the object resting on the table, hook the spring scale to it. Do not stretch the spring.
>
> Pull the object smoothly across the table. Do not jerk the object. If you pull with a jerky motion, the spring scale will wiggle too much for you to get a good reading.
>
> As you are pulling, read the number of newtons you are using to pull the object.

Making a Spring Scale

If you do not have a spring scale, you can make one by following the directions below.

DO THIS

1 Staple one end of the rubber band (the part with the sharp curve) to the middle of one end of the cardboard so that the rubber band hangs down the length of the cardboard. Color the loose end of the rubber band with a marker to make it easy to see.

2 Bend the paper clip so that it is slightly open and forms a hook. Hang the paper clip by its unopened end from the rubber band.

3 Put the narrow paper strip across the rubber band, and staple the strip to the cardboard. The rubber band and hook must be able to move easily.

4 While holding the cardboard upright, hang one 100-g mass from the hook. Allow the mass to come to rest, and mark the position of the bottom of the rubber band on the cardboard. Label this position on the cardboard 1 N. Add another 100-g mass for a total of 200 g.

5 Continue to add masses and mark the cardboard. Each 100-g mass adds a force of about 1 N.

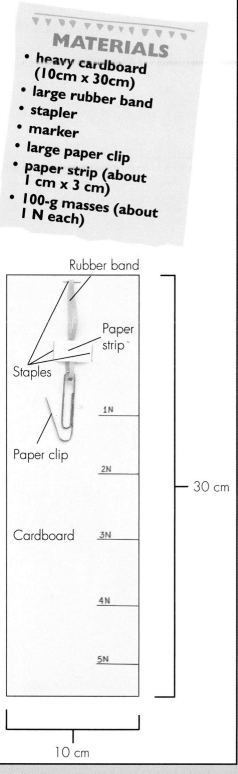

Rubber band

Paper strip

Staples

Paper clip

1 N

2 N

Cardboard

3 N

4 N

5 N

30 cm

10 cm

Working Like a Scientist
What Do Rabbits Like to Eat?

Have you ever wanted to know about something but you didn't know how to find out about it? Working like a scientist can help. Read the story below to find out how Alita, Juan, and Jasmine learned to work like scientists.

Alita, Juan, and Jasmine were friends. Each of them owned a rabbit. "I'd like to give my rabbit a treat," Alita told Juan and Jasmine. "I want the treat to be something that my rabbit likes. It should also be good for the rabbit."

"What do you think the best treat would be?" Juan asked.

"That's a good question," Jasmine said. "How can we find out the answer?"

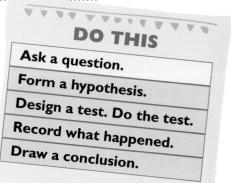

DO THIS

Ask a question.

Form a hypothesis.

Design a test. Do the test.

Record what happened.

Draw a conclusion.

Asking a good question is the first step in working like a scientist. A good question helps you find out what the problem is. A good question starts you on the way to finding an answer. Often a good question will have many answers.

After you ask a good question, you need to choose one possible answer and then find out if your answer is right. This possible answer to your question is called a *hypothesis.* You *form a hypothesis* when you choose an answer to a question. Sometimes you must do research before you can choose an answer. Find out how Alita, Juan, and Jasmine formed their hypothesis.

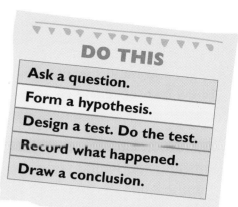

DO THIS

Ask a question.

Form a hypothesis.

Design a test. Do the test.

Record what happened.

Draw a conclusion.

The next day, Alita, Juan, and Jasmine met at Alita's house. Juan and Jasmine had brought their rabbits in their carrying cages.

"We need to find out what the best treat for a rabbit would be," Juan said.

Alita said, "My grandpa told me that rabbits like all kinds of vegetables. Maybe vegetables would be the best treat."

"I gave my rabbit some celery once and she didn't eat it at all. I wonder if my rabbit is different," Juan replied.

Jasmine said, "Why don't we say that we think rabbits like carrots, celery, and broccoli? Then we could test our rabbits to see if we're right."

"Yes," Alita said. "We can offer each rabbit carrots, celery, and broccoli and see what each one likes best."

"That sounds like a good idea," Juan said.

When Jasmine said to *do a test*, she was talking about doing an experiment. An experiment must be carefully designed and planned. You must decide how to do your test and how to record the results.

Alita said, "We can put the three kinds of vegetables in each cage. We can watch our rabbits and see which vegetables they eat."

Jasmine said, "But we should do the test when we know our rabbits aren't very hungry. If they were, they might eat anything. I know that when I'm very hungry, I eat anything."

"That's true," Juan said. "And we shouldn't put one vegetable closer to the rabbit than the other vegetables. The rabbit might eat the first vegetable it saw. It might not eat the vegetable it liked best."

Alita said, "That sounds good. Let me write that down."

DO THIS

| Ask a question. |
| Form a hypothesis. |
| Design a test. Do the test. |
| Record what happened. |
| Draw a conclusion. |

Jasmine said, "I've been thinking about our test. How are we going to know what the answer is? We should be able to say why we're giving our rabbits a certain kind of treat."

Juan said, "That's a good question. We have to find a way to record what our rabbits do."

Alita smiled. She showed Juan and Jasmine a chart.

"I made up this chart. It has a place for each rabbit and each kind of vegetable. We can see which vegetable each rabbit eats first."

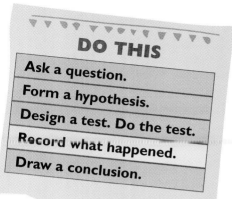

DO THIS

| Ask a question. |
| Form a hypothesis. |
| Design a test. Do the test. |
| Record what happened. |
| Draw a conclusion. |

A Rabbit's Favorite Treat								
	Broccoli			Carrots			Celery		
	1st	2nd	3rd	1st	2nd	3rd	1st	2nd	3rd
Jasmine's Rabbit									
Juan's Rabbit									
Alita's Rabbit									

What Alita showed Juan and Jasmine was a way to record what they saw the rabbits do. This is called *recording data.* It is an important part of science because it helps you explain why you think one answer may be right and another may be wrong.

Alita, Juan, and Jasmine put broccoli, carrots, and celery into the three rabbit cages. Alita's rabbit smelled the broccoli and then hopped to the carrots.

The rabbit ate some of the carrots, but it did not eat the celery. Jasmine's rabbit ate the carrots and a little bit of the celery. Juan's rabbit ate only the carrots.

Alita filled in the chart, and the three friends looked at it. Jasmine said, "It looks as if all three rabbits like carrots. My rabbit likes celery. None of the rabbits like broccoli."

DO THIS

Ask a question.
Form a hypothesis.
Design a test. Do the test.
Record what happened.
Draw a conclusion.

A Rabbit's Favorite Treat	Broccoli			Carrots			Celery		
	1st	2nd	3rd	1st	2nd	3rd	1st	2nd	3rd
Jasmine's Rabbit				X				X	
Juan's Rabbit				X					
Alita's Rabbit				X					

What Jasmine did is *draw a conclusion.* She looked at the results of the test and was able to say what she thought the test showed. Just doing a test is not enough. You must be able to say what the test showed you.

"We haven't tried all vegetables," Juan said.

"No," Alita said. "And we didn't measure how much of the carrots and celery Jasmine's rabbit ate."

"We can do more tests," Jasmine said.

"All right," Alita said. "That would be fun!"

Juan said, "But for now, we know that our rabbits like carrots. So we can give them carrots for treats."

INDEX

Note: Page numbers in italics indicate illustrations.

Axis, Earth's, *B19*, B78
Axle, *C56*
    See also Wheels and axles

Baboons, *A56*
Backbone
    activity, A44
    animals with, *A43–A47*
    animals without,
      A48–A49
Bacteria, *D61*
Baden-Powell, B. F. S.,
    E46–E47
Balance, *C15*, *C79*, *R10*, *R11*
Balancing (Jennings), C9
Ballonets (blimp), *E36–E37*
Ballonet valves, *E36–E37*
Balloon, *B43*, *B46*, *E12*
    weight of air in, B43
    See also Hot-air balloon;
      Weather balloon
Bare, Colleen Stanley, A9
Bar magnets, *C20–C21*
Barometer, *B46*, *B47*, *B48*, *B49*,
    B50, *B51*, *B52*, *B53*
    activities, B46–B47,
      B52–B53
    defined, B78
    development of, B48–B51
    kinds of, B51
    uses of, B48
Basket (hot-air balloon), *E32*
Beagle, *A13*
Beaker, *R7*
Beaks
    activity, A26–A27
    of birds, A26–A27, *A29*
    of a falcon, *A47*
Beams, Bill, *B55–B57*
Bear, *A66*
Beavers, A15, *D42*
Bengal tiger, *A24*
Bernoulli, Daniel, E23
Biplanes, *E2–E3*
Birds, *A3*, *A12*, A15, *A29*, A36,
    A43, A54, *A94*

beaks of, A26–A27, *A29*,
    A47
behavior of, A54
camouflage of, A94
classifying, A40, *A43*, *A45*,
    A47
eggs of, A79
feathers of, A17
in freshwater ecosystem,
    D18, D42, D46
migration of, A60–A64
nesting of, A15
spine of, A43
Bison, A70, *A71*, *B3*
Bjork, Christina, B9
Blimps, E26, E34–E37, *E35*,
    E36–E37
    parts of, E36–E37
    uses of, E35
Bluegills, *D14*
Blue heron, *D18*
Boa constrictor, *A74*
Body coverings, A16–A20,
    A16, *A17*, *A20*
Bogong moths, *A95*
Boring, Mel, C68–C71
Botswana, *D28–D29*
Bottle opener, *C54*
Brain, effects of pollution on,
    B67
Breathing, A14–A15
Bridges, *C3*, *C6*, *C30–C33*
    activity, C72–C73
    types of, C30–C33
Bridges (Robbins), C9
*Bridge That Couldn't Be Built,
The* (Boring), C68–C71
Brook, *D54*
Brooklyn Bridge (NY), *C3*
Brown, Ken, E8
Bucket wheel excavator,
    C65
Bullfrog, *D29*
Burner (hot-air balloon), E32,
    E33
Buson, E18
Busy Busy Squirrels (Bare), A9
Butterfly
    from egg, *A88–A89*
    migration of, *A60*

Cable, *C57*
CALTRANS, C66
Camel, *A32*
Camouflage, *A23*, *A24*, *A94*
    as defense, *A23–A24*
    defined, A23, A94
Camp Springs (MD), B56
Canada, *B25*
Canada geese, activity,
    A62–A63
Canadian musk oxen, *A56*
Canis familiaris, A42
Can opener, *C23*, *C64*, *C78*
Can Rain Be Dangerous?,
    B69–B73
Cantilever bridge, *C33*
Carapace, *A34*
Careers
    bird sanctuary worker, *A64*
    environmentalist,
      D72–D73
    heavy-equipment
      operator, C66–C67
    meteorologist, E70–E71
    weather reporter, B6
    weather researcher, B7
    weather scientist, B55–B57
Carolina Sandhills National
    Wildlife Refuge, A62–A63
Carter, Gale, *E70–E71*
Cartoon (*Calvin and
    Hobbes*), x
Cat, *A80–A83*
Catfish, *D15*
Celsius temperature, R8
Chandra, Deborah, E19
Chemicals, as pollutants,
    B60, *B70*
Cherry, Lynne, D9
Chicken, *A75*, *A79*
Cirrus clouds, *B33*, *B78*
Clam, *A49*
Clarke, Barry, D9
Classifying, A10, A39, A85
    reasons for, A37
    scientific, A40–A41

ACKNOWLEDGMENTS

For permission to reprint copyrighted material, grateful acknowledgment is made to the following sources:

Mel Boring: From "The Bridge That Couldn't Be Built" in *Cricket* Magazine, June 1991. Text © by Mel Boring.

Carolrhoda Books, Inc., Minneapolis, MN: Cover illustration from *How the Guinea Fowl Got Her Spots* by Barbara Knutson. Copyright © 1990 by Barbara Knutson.

Children's Better Health Institute, Indianapolis, IN: From "Magic Jumpson" (originally titled "The Froggie") in *Jack and Jill* Magazine, March 1991. Text copyright © 1988 by Children's Better Health Institute, Benjamin Franklin Literary & Medical Society, Inc.

Coward, McCann & Geoghegan: Abridged from "Amelia Earhart" by Peggy Mann in *Amelia Earhart, First Lady of Flight.* Text copyright © 1970 by Peggy Mann.

Current Health 1® Magazine: "Can Rain Be Dangerous?" from *Current Health 1®* Magazine, November 1991. Text copyright © 1991 by Weekly Reader Corporation. Published by Weekly Reader Corporation.

Dial Books for Young Readers, a division of Penguin Books USA Inc.: Cover illustration from *Bridges* by Ken Robbins. Copyright © 1991 by Ken Robbins.

Doubleday, a division of Bantam Doubleday Dell Publishing Group, Inc.: Cover illustration from *Why Can't I Fly?* by Ken Brown. Copyright © 1990 by Ken Brown.

Dutton Children's Books, a division of Penguin Books USA Inc.: From *It's an Armadillo!* by Bianca Lavies. Copyright © 1989 by Bianca Lavies.

Farrar, Straus & Giroux, Inc.: "Ribbons of Wind" from *Balloons and Other Poems* by Deborah Chandra. Text copyright © 1988, 1990 by Deborah Chandra.

Frank Fretz: Illustration by Frank Fretz from "Only the Tough Survive" by James Halfpenny in *Ranger Rick* Magazine, December 1993.

Harcourt Brace & Company: Cover illustration from *A River Ran Wild* by Lynne Cherry. Copyright © 1992 by Lynne Cherry.

The Hokuseido Press, Tokyo, Japan: Untitled haiku (Retitled: "Japanese Poem") by Buson from *Haiku*, Vols. 1-4, translated by R. H. Blyth.

Holiday House, Inc.: Cover illustration from *Weather Words and What They Mean* by Gail Gibbons. Copyright © 1990 by Gail Gibbons.

Richard Lewis: Untitled poem (Retitled: "African Bushman Poem") from *Out of the Earth I Sing*, edited by Richard Lewis. Text copyright © 1968 by Richard Lewis.

Little, Brown and Company: From *Four Corners of the Sky: Poems, Chants and Oratory* (Retitled: "Native American Kiowa Verse"), selected by Theodore Clymer. Text copyright © 1975 by Theodore Clymer.

Little, Brown and Company, in Association with Arcade Publishing, Inc.: Cover illustration by Ted Rand from *Water's Way* by Lisa Westberg Peters. Illustration copyright © 1991 by Ted Rand.

Lothrop, Lee & Shepard Books, a division of William Morrow & Company, Inc.: Cover illustration by Catherine Stock from *Galimoto* by Karen Lynn Williams. Illustration copyright © 1990 by Catherine Stock.

National Wildlife Federation: "Amazing Jumping Machine" by Carolyn Duckworth from *Ranger Rick* Magazine, March 1991. Text copyright 1991 by the National Wildlife Federation. "Only the Tough Survive" by James Halfpenny from *Ranger Rick* Magazine, December 1993. Text copyright 1993 by the National Wildlife Federation. Drawings by Jack Shepherd from "Magic Jumpson" in *Ranger Rick* Magazine, March 1991. Copyright 1991 by the National Wildlife Federation.

North-South Books Inc., New York: Cover illustration from *The Air Around Us* by Eleonore Schmid. Copyright © 1992 by Nord-Sud Verlag AG, Gossau Zürich, Switzerland.

Marian Reiner: Untitled haiku (Retitled: "Japanese Poem") by Asayasu from *More Cricket Songs*, translated by Harry Behn. Text copyright © 1971 by Harry Behn.

Sierra Club Books for Children: From *Come Back, Salmon* by Molly Cone. Text copyright © 1992 by Molly Cone.

Simon & Schuster Books for Young Readers, New York: Cover illustration from *Frog Odyssey* by Juliet and Charles Snape. © 1991 by Juliet and Charles Snape.

Gareth Stevens, Inc., Milwaukee, WI: From *Rockets, Probes, and Satellites* by Isaac Asimov. Text © 1988 by Nightfall, Inc.

Walker and Company: Cover illustration by Valerie A. Kells from *One Earth, a Multitude of Creatures* by Peter and Connie Roop. Illustration copyright © 1992 by Valerie A. Kells.

PHOTO CREDITS
Key: (t)top, (b)bottom, (l)left, (r)right, (c)center, (bg)background.

Front Cover, All Other Photographs: (tl), Robert Maier/Animals Animals; (tr), NASA/International Stock Photo; (c), Jean-Francois Causse/Tony Stone Images; (cr), Kristian Hilsen/Tony Stone Images; (bl), Benn Mitchell/The Image Bank; (br), E.R. Degginger/Color-Pic.
Back Cover, Harcourt Brace & Company Photographs: (t), Greg Leary; (bl), Earl Kogler.
Back Cover, All Other Photographs: (br), Kaz Mori/The Image Bank.
To The Student, Harcourt Brace & Company Photographs: vi(tr), vi(c), Weronica Ankarorn; vi(b), Maria Paraskevas; viii, Earl Kogler; xv(b), Jerry White.
To The Student, All Other Photographs: iv(tl), Neena Wilmot/Stock/Art Images; iv(tr), Jane Burton/Bruce Coleman, Inc.; iv(bl), Dwight R. Kuhn; iv(br), Dave B. Fleetham/Tom Stack & Assoc.; v(t), Dave Bartruff; v(b), Photri; vi(tl), W. Hille/Leo de Wys, Inc.; vii(l), Stephen Dalton/Photo Researchers; vii(r), John Gerlach/Tom Stack & Assoc.; x, David Young-Wolff/PhotoEdit; xi(t), T. Rosenthal/SuperStock; xi(b), Gabe Palmer/The Stock Market; xii, Myrleen Ferguson Cate/PhotoEdit; xiii, Tony Freeman/PhotoEdit; xiv(l), Jeff Greenberg/Photo Researchers; xiv(r), Russell D. Curtis/Photo Researchers; xv(t), Bob Daemmrich; xvi(l), Myrleen Ferguson Cate/PhotoEdit; xvi(r), Bob Daemmrich/Stock, Boston.
Unit A, Harcourt Brace & Company Photographs: A4-A5, A6(t), A7, Dick Krueger; A8, A9, Weronica Ankarorn; A10-A11, Dick Krueger; A16(r), A17(tr), A17(b), A19, A20(b), A22, A27, A37, A38, A43(l), A44, Earl Kogler; A63, Eric Camden; A76, A86, Earl Kogler; A92-A93(bg), David Lavine; A92(t), A93, Earl Kogler.
Unit A, All Other Photographs: Unit Page Divider, Erwin & Peggy Bauer; A1, A2-A3, Alan & Sandy Carey; A3, Hugh P. Smith, Jr.; A6(b), Alan Briere/SuperStock; A12(bg), Index Stock; A12(t), David R. Frazier; A12(b), William Johnson/Stock, Boston; A13(t), Henry Ausloos/Animals Animals; A13(b), Antoinette

Jongen/SuperStock; A14(t), John Cancalosi/Stock, Boston; A14(b), M. Bruce/SuperStock; A15(t), Stephen G. Maka/Lightwave; A15(b), H. Lanks/SuperStock; A16(l), G. Corbett/SuperStock; A17(tl), Stephen J. Krasemann/NHPA; A20(t), M. Burgess/SuperStock; A21, A. Mercieca/SuperStock; A23(t), Dwight R. Kuhn; A23(b), James T. Jones/David R. Frazier Photolibrary; A24(t), SuperStock; A24(b), Stephen G. Maka/Lightwave; A25(t), Gary Bell/The Wildlife Collection; A25(cl), Larry A. Brazil; A25(cr), Stephen J. Krasemann/Valan Photos; A25(b), David Cavagnaro/Peter Arnold, Inc.; A28, The Granger Collection; A30(tl), A. Kaiser/SuperStock; A30(tr), Stephen Dalton/NHPA; A30(b), Aaron Haupt/David R. Frazier Photolibrary; A31, A32(t), SuperStock; A32(c), John Giustina/The Wildlife Collection; A32(b), Sven-Olaf Lindblad/Photo Researchers; A33(t), A33(b), A34(t), A34(c), A34(b), A35(l), A35(r), Bianca Lavies; A36(bg), Rod Planck/Tony Stone Images; A36(t), Scot Stewart; A36(b), Stephen G. Maka/Lightwave; A39(tl), Bill Tronca/Tom Stack & Assoc.; A39(tc), A39(tr), T. Wolf Bolz/TexStockPhotoInc.; A39(bl), David M. Dennis/Tom Stack & Assoc.; A39(bc), Claudio Ferer/Devaney Stock Photos; A39(br) Gerald & Buff Corsi/Tom Stack & Assoc.; A40, Leonard Lee Rue III/Animals Animals; A41, Tetsu Yamazaki; A42, Bob Daemmrich/The Image Works; A43(r), Don Enger/Animals Animals; A45(l), Ron & Valerie Taylor/Bruce Coleman, Inc.; A45(r), A46(t), Zig Leszczynski/Animals Animals; A46(cl), E.R. Degginger/Color-Pic; A46(cr), Renee Lynn/Photo Researchers; A46(b), Holton Collection/SuperStock; A47(tl), Alan G. Nelson/Animals Animals; A47(tr), E.R. Degginger/Animals Animals; A47(c), Fred Whitehead/Animals Animals; A47(b), Dominique Braud/Tom Stack & Assoc.; A48(t), Brian Parker/Tom Stack & Assoc.; A48(b), Oxford Scientific Films/Animals Animals; A49(tl), Dwight R. Kuhn; A49(tc), Lester V. Bergman & Assoc.; A49(tr), Rod Planck/Tom Stack & Assoc.; A49(cl), Biophoto Associates/Photo Researchers; A49(cr), John Shaw/Tom Stack & Assoc.; A49(b), Dave B. Fleetham/Tom Stack & Assoc.; A52(bg), Tim Fitzharris/Masterfile; A52(t) H. Morton/SuperStock; A52(b), John Cancalosi/Valan Photos; A53, D. Robert Franz/The Wildlife Collection; A54(tl), Stephen G. Maka/Lightwave; A54(tr), Hank Andrews/Visuals Unlimited; A54(b), Mike Bacon/Tom Stack & Assoc.; A55(t), Stephen G. Maka/Lightwave; A55(b), SuperStock; A56(t), Stephen G. Maka/Lightwave; A56(c), Gerald & Buff Corsi/Tom Stack & Assoc.; A56(b), Fred Bruemmer/Valan Photos; A57(t), Scot Stewart; A57(b), Western History Department/Denver Public Library; A58(tl), A58(tr), Daniel W. Gotshall; A58(bl) SuperStock; A58(br), Dwight R. Kuhn; A59(t), SuperStock; A59(b), John Cancalosi/Valan Photos; A61(t), M. Bruce/SuperStock; A61(b), SuperStock; A62-A63(bg), Index Stock; A64(t) A64(b) Master's Studio; A65, Jane Burton/Bruce Coleman, Inc.; A66, Mark Sherman/Bruce Coleman, Inc.; A67, Michael S. Quinton; A68(t), Erwin & Peggy Bauer; A68(bl), Frank Fretz; A68(br), Erwin & Peggy Bauer; A69, Stephen J. Krasemann/DRK; A70, Leonard Lee Rue III; A71, Erwin & Peggy Bauer; A72(bg), Gregory Dimijian/Photo Researchers; A72(t), John Colwell/Grant Heilman Photography; A72(b), H. Mark Weidman; A73, David R. Frazier; A74(t), Allen Russell/ProFiles West; A74(c), Doug Perrine/Innerspace Visions; A74(b), John Cancalosi/Tom Stack & Assoc.; A75(t), John Fowler/Valan Photos; A75(cl), Dwight R. Kuhn; A75(cr), Stephen G. Maka/Lightwave; A75(b), Martin Harvey/The Wildlife Collection; A77, Wolfgang Kaehler; A78(t), Dr. Paul V. Loiselle; A78(b), John T. Pennington/Ivy Images; A79, Martin Harvey/The Wildlife Collection; A80, A81(t), A81(b), A82(t), A82(cl), A82(cr), A82(b), A83(t), Dwight R. Kuhn; A83(bl), A83(br), Renee Stockdale/Animals Animals; A84(tl), Dwight R. Kuhn; A84(tr), Tom & Pat Leeson/DRK; A84(bl), Mella

Panzella/Animals Animals; A84(br), Neena Wilmot/Stock/Art Images; A85(tl), Gary Braasch; A85(tr), Brian Parker/Tom Stack & Assoc.; A85(cl), A85(c), SuperStock; A85(cr), Gary Braasch; A85(b), A88(t), A88(cl), A88(cr), A88(b), A89(l), A89(r), Dwight R. Kuhn; A90-A91, Index Stock; A91(l), SuperStock; A91(r), A. Briere/SuperStock; A92(b), Allen Russell/ProFiles West; A94(t), Sven-Olaf Lindblad/Photo Researchers; A94(c), Anthony J. Bond/Valan Photos; A94(b), Stephen J. Krasemann/Valan Photos; A95(l), Wolfgang Bayer/Bruce Coleman, Inc.; A95(r), A. Mercieca/SuperStock.

Unit B, Harcourt Brace & Company Photographs: B4-B5, B6(t), B7(t), B7(b), Dick Krueger; B8, B9, Weronica Ankarorn; B10-B11, Maria Paraskevas; B14, B15, B16, B17, B20, Earl Kogler; B23(cb), Rodney Jones; B28(bc), B29(t), B29(b), B30, B36, B37, Earl Kogler; B40(bg), David Phillips; B41, B42, Earl Kogler; B43, Richard Nowitz; B44, B46(t), B46(b), B47, B53, Earl Kogler; B55(t), B55(b), B56(l), B56(r), B57, Jerry Heasley; B61, B63, B68, Richard T. Nowitz; B76(t), B76(b), Earl Kogler; B77(b), Richard T. Nowitz; 79(t), Earl Kogler.

Unit B, All Other Photographs: Unit Page Divider, A. Farquhar/Valan Photos; B1, Amy Drutman; B2-3, Gordon Wiltsie/Peter Arnold, Inc.; B3, Alan & Sandy Carey; B6(c), R. Dahlquist/SuperStock; B6(b), George Cargill/Lightwave; B12(bg), Jay Maisel; B12, Scott Barrow; B18(l), B18(r), B19(l), B19(r), E.R. Degginger/Bruce Coleman, Inc.; B22(t), SuperStock; B22(ct), David R. Frazier; B22(cb), Scott Barrow; B22(b), Hans & Judy Beste/Earth Scenes; B23(t), Scott Barrow; B23(ct), Harry M. Walker; B23(b), Loren McIntyre; B24(tl), Will & Deni McIntyre/AllStock; B24(tr), Tony Freeman/PhotoEdit; B24(cl), J.C. Carton/Bruce Coleman, Inc.; B24(cr), Richard T. Nowitz; B24(b), Fotoconcept; B25(t), John Eastcott, Yva Momatiuk/Valan Photos; B25(b), Sovfoto; B27, David Falconer/David R. Frazier Photolibrary; B28(bg), Dwight R. Kuhn; B28(t), Steve Solum/Bruce Coleman, Inc.; B28(bl), David R. Frazier; B28(br), Dave Bartruff; B32-B33, Gary Black/Masterfile; B32, Peter Griffith/Masterfile; B33, Mark Tomalty/Masterfile; B34, Peter Miller/Photo Researchers; B35(t), Alan Hicks/AllStock; B35(c), Wouterloot-Gregoire/Valan Photos; B35(b), Joyce Photographics/Valan Photos; B36-B37(bg), Dick Thomas/Visuals Unlimited; B40(t), Phil Degginger/Color-Pic; B40(b), Tony Freeman/PhotoEdit; B48, The Granger Collection; B50(bg), John Running/Stock, Boston; B50, The Granger Collection; B51(t) David R. Frazier; B51(b), Photri; B52, Runk, Schoenberger/Grant Heilman Photography; B54(l), A. Farquhar/Valan Photos; B54(r), SuperStock; B58(bg), David Woodfall/Tony Stone Images; B58(t), E.R. Degginger/Color-Pic; B58(b), Jose L. Pelaez/The Stock Market; B59, R. Llewellyn/SuperStock; B60(t), E.R. Degginger/Color-Pic; B60(c), Tony Freeman/PhotoEdit; B60(b), Anna Zuckerman/PhotoEdit; B62-B63(bg), E.R. Degginger/Color-Pic; B64, B65, B66, David R. Frazier; B67, Tony Freeman/PhotoEdit; B69, Ruth Dixon; B70, North Wind; B71, Phil Degginger/Color-Pic; B72(t), Bill Weedmark; B72(b), Dave Bartruff; B73, Grapes Michaud/Photo Researchers; B74-B75, J.R. Page/Valan Photos; B75(t), Valerie Wilkinson/Valan Photos; B75(b), SuperStock; B76-B77(bg), Greg Vaughn/Tom Stack & Assoc.; B77(t), Aaron Haupt/David R. Frazier Photolibrary; B78(t), Runk, Schoenberger/Grant Heilman Photography; B78(b), Mark Tomalty/Masterfile; B79(c) Gary Black/Masterfile; B79(b), John Heseltine/Photo Researchers; B80(l), Peter Griffith/Masterfile; B80(r), A. Upitis/SuperStock.

Unit C, Harcourt Brace & Company Photographs: C4-C5, C6(c), C6(b), C7(t), David Phillips; C7(c), Earl Kogler; C7(b), David Phillips; C8, C9, Weronica Ankarorn; C10-C11, C13, C14(b), C15(t), C15(bl), C15(br), C16, C17, C19(tl), C19(tr), C19(b), Earl Kogler; C20-C21(bg), Jerry White; C20, C21(t), C21(bl), C21(br),

C22(tr), C22(br), C23(tl), C23(c), C23(b), C24, C25, C28(l), C28(c), C28(r), C29(t), C29(b), Earl Kogler; C32(t), Gerald Ratto; C35, Earl Kogler; C36, C37, C39, C40, C43(t), C43(c), C43(b), C45(t), Dick Krueger; C45(b), Rob Downey; C46-C47(bg), Dick Krueger; C46, C47, Weronica Ankarorn; C48, Dick Krueger; C52(b), C53, Maria Paraskevas; C54(t), Bruce Wilson; C54(cl), Weronica Ankarorn; C54(cr), Earl Kogler; C54(b), Weronica Ankarorn; C55, Earl Kogler; C56(t), C56(b), C57(t), Maria Paraskevas; C58, Earl Kogler; C59(t), C59(b), Maria Paraskevas; C60, C61, C63(t), C63(b), C64, Earl Kogler; C66(t), C66(b), C67, Robert Landau; C73, C75(t), Earl Kogler; C75(b), David Phillips; C76(t), Earl Kogler; C76(b), David Phillips; C77, Jerry White; C78(l), Earl Kogler; C79(tl), Bruce Wilson; C79(tr), Earl Kogler; C79(bl), David Phillips; C79(br), Earl Kogler.

Unit C, All Other Photographs: Unit Page Divider, Bud Nielsen/Lightwave; C1, Richard T. Nowitz/Valan Photos; C2-C3, David R. Frazier; C3, Rapho/Photo Researchers; C6(t), SuperStock; C12(bg), Harold Sund/The Image Bank; C12(t), James Blank/Zephyr Pictures; C12(b), W. Hille/Leo de Wys, Inc.; C14(t), Terry Wild Studio; C14(c), Ewing Galloway; C22(l), T. Matsumoto/Sygma; C23(tr), E.R. Degginger/Earth Scenes; C24-C25(bg), NASA; C26, The Bettmann Archive; C27, Lewis Portnoy/Spectra-Action; C30, Christopher Liu/ChinaStock; C31(t), Milt & Joan Mann/Cameramann; C31(b), Harry M. Walker; C32(b), Robert Frerck/Odyssey Productions; C33, Yves Tessier/Tessima; C34(bg), Roy Ooms/Masterfile; C34(t), John Terence Turner/FPG; C34(b), Alissa Crandall; C38-C39(bg), SuperStock; C41, Paul Souders/AllStock; C42(t), David R. Frazier; C42(c), C42(b), Alan & Sandy Carey; C44, NASA/Photri; C49, Dave Bartruff; C50-C51(bg), William Warren/West Light; C50(all), C51(all), Insurance Institute for Highway Safety; C52(bg), Index Stock; C52(t), Bud Nielsen/Lightwave; C57(b), Neena M. Wilmot/Stock/Art Images; C62(t), Ruth Dixon; C62(c), Dave Bartruff; C62(b), Aldo Mastrocola/Lightwave; C68, Steinman, Boynton, Gronquist & Birdsall; C70-C71, Frederic Stein/FPG; C72-C73(bg), Ken Graham; C74-C75(bg), SuperStock; C76-C77(bg), Andrew Sacks/Tony Stone Images; C78(r), Lewis Portony/Spectra-Action.

Unit D, Harcourt Brace & Company Photographs: D4-D5, Earl Kogler; D6(t), Dick Krueger; D8, D9, Weronica Ankarorn; D10-D11, D22, D23(b), Britt Runion; D24, Earl Kogler; D25, D26-D27, Britt Runion; D37(t), D37(b), D60(t), D62(t), D62(b) D63, D64, D65, Earl Kogler; D72, D73, Robert Landau; D76, D77(t), Richard T. Nowitz; D77(b), Earl Kogler.

Unit D, All Other Photographs: Unit Page Divider, Mark J. Thomas/Dembinsky Photo Assoc; D1, D2-D3, Larry Lefever/Grant Heilman Photography; D3, Adam Jones/Dembinsky Photo Assoc.; D6(b), William McKinney/FPG; D7, Neena M. Wilmot/Stock/Art Images; D12(bg), Greg Nikas/Viesti Assoc.; D12(t), David R. Frazier; D12(b), Ruth Dixon; D13, Rod Planck/Tom Stack & Assoc.; D14(t), M.P.L. Fogden/Bruce Coleman, Inc.; D14(b), E.R. Degginger/Bruce Coleman, Inc.; D15(t), S. Maimone/SuperStock; D15(b), John Gerlach/Tom Stack & Assoc.; D16-D17(bg), Gabe Palmer/The Stock Market; D16, Gary Meszaros/Dembinsky Photo Assoc.; D17, John Shaw/Bruce Coleman, Inc.; D18(t), Mark J. Thomas/Dembinsky Photo Assoc.; D18(b), J.H. Robinson/Photo Researchers; D19, Gay Bumgarner/Photo Network; D23(t), Patti Murray/Earth Scenes; D28-D29, Betsy Blass/Photo Researchers; D29(tl), Karl H. Switak/Photo Researchers; D29(tr), E.R. Degginger/Color-Pic; D30(bg), Stephen G. Maka/Lightwave; D30(t), Stephen Dalton/Photo Researchers; D30(b), Stephen J. Krasemann/Valan Photos; D31, Stephen Dalton/Photo Researchers; D32(t), Zig Leszczynski/Animals Animals; D32(c), J.H. Robinson/Animals Animals; D32(b), Zig Leszczynski/Animals Animals; D33(t), Kim Taylor/Bruce Coleman, Inc.; D33(b), Gregory Dimijian/Photo Researchers; D38(t), D38(b), D39(t), D39(c), D39(b), Dwight R. Kuhn; D44(bg), SuperStock; D44(t), P. Van Rhijn/SuperStock; D44(b), Bob & Clara Calhoun/Bruce Coleman, Inc.; D46, D47 Dwight R. Kuhn; D48(t), Mildred McPhee/Valan Photos; D48(cl), Bill Beatty/Wild & Natural; D48(cr), E.R. Degginger/Color-Pic; D48(cb), Glen D. Chambers; D48(bl), J. Faircloth/Transparencies; D48(br), Oxford Scientific Films/Animals Animals; D49(t), J.A. Wilkinson/Valan Photos; D49(cl), Bill Beatty/Wild & Natural; D49(cr), Steve Maslowski/Valan Photos; D49(cb), Thomas Kitchin/Tom Stack & Assoc.; D49((bl), Bill Beatty/Wild & Natural; D49(br), John Shaw/Bruce Coleman, Inc.; D54, Phillip Norton/Valan Photos; D56-D57, Manley/SuperStock; D56, John Eastcott, Yva Momatiuk/Stock, Boston; D58(bg), R. Dahlquist/SuperStock; D58(t), M. Roessler/SuperStock; D58(b), D59, SuperStock; D60(b), Mark E. Gibson; D61(t), Dwight R. Kuhn; D61(b), A. Hennek/SuperStock; D66, D67(t), D67(b), D68, D69, D70(tl), D70(tr), D70(b), Sidnee Wheelwright; D71(t), Chris Huss/The Wildlife Collection; D71(c), D71(b), Sidnee Wheelwright; D74-D75(bg), SuperStock; D75, Nancy Sefton/Photo Researchers; D76-D77(bg), Andy Caulfield/The Image Bank; D78, James H. Carmichael, Jr./The Image Bank.

Unit E, Harcourt Brace & Company Photographs: E4-E5, Weronica Ankarorn; E6(t), Earl Kogler; E6(b), Dick Krueger; E8, E9, Weronica Ankarorn; E10-E11, E13, E14(t), E14(b), E15, Earl Kogler; E16, Weronica Ankarorn; E17, E20, E23, E24, E27, E29, E30, E38(t), E41(t), E41(b), E50, E57, E61, Earl Kogler; E91(r), Dick Krueger; E92(t), Earl Kogler; E92(b), Maria Paraskevas; E93, Dick Krueger.

Unit E, All Other Photographs: Unit Page Divider, Frank P. Rossotto/The Stock Market; E1, E2-E3, Neena M. Wilmot/Stock/Art Images; E2, Archiv/Photo Researchers; E3, Frank P. Rossotto/The Stock Market; E7, Milt & Joan Mann/Cameramann; E12(bg), Craig Aurness/West Light; E12(t), Allen S. Stone/Devaney Stock Photos; E12(b), Kennon Cooke/Valan Photos; E21, Wide World Photos; E26(bg), M. Stephenson/West Light; E26(t), K. Sklute/SuperStock; E26(b) North Wind; E30-E31(bg), Alese & Mort Pechter/The Stock Market; E33, Ron Watts/Black Star; E35, Linc Cornell/Light Sources; E38(bg), J.A. Kraulis/Masterfile; E38(b), Norman Owen Tomalin/Bruce Coleman, Inc.; E40(t), Russ Kinne/Comstock; E40(b), Spencer Swanger/Tom Stack & Assoc.; E47, William Carter/Photo Researchers; E54(bg), Paul Chesley/Tony Stone Images; E54(t), Steve Kaufman/Ken Graham Agency; E54(b), UPI/Bettmann; E55(tl), Percy Jones/Archive Photos; E55(tr), Photri; E55(c), Charles Palek/Tom Stack & Assoc.; E55(bl), Photri; E55(br), Frank P. Rossotto/Tom Stack & Assoc.; E60(l), Richard P. Smith/Tom Stack & Assoc.; E60(r), Ken Gouvin/Comstock; E62, Gerald & Buff Corsi/Tom Stack & Assoc.; E63(t), Gary Benson/Comstock; E63(b), John McDermott/Tony Stone Images; E64(t), Neena M. Wilmot/Stock/Art Images; E64(b), John Shaw/Tom Stack & Assoc.; E65, Bruce Matheson/PHOTO/NATS; E66, Archive Photos; E67, UPI/Bettmann Newsphotos; E68, The Bettmann Archive; E70, E71, U.S. Air Force; E72(bg), NASA; E72(t), NASA/Photri; E72(b), E78, NASA; E79, J. Novak/SuperStock; E80(t), Hank Brandli and Rob Downey; E80(b), European Space Agency/Photo Researchers; E81, David R. Frazier; E82, NASA/Photri; E84, E86(t), E86(c), NASA; E86(b), E87(t), Frank P. Rossotto/Tom Stack & Assoc.; E87(c), NASA; E87(b), W. Kaufmann/Photo Researchers; E88(tl), NASA; E88(tr), E88(c), E88(bl), E88(br), NASA/Photri; E89(t), NASA; E89(b), NASA/Photri; E90-E91(bg), Wendy Shattil, Bob Rozinski/Tom Stack & Assoc.; E91(l), NASA; E92-E93(bg), Greg Vaughn/Tom Stack & Assoc.; E94, Gerald & Buff Corsi/Tom Stack & Assoc.; E95, NASA.